PASTORAL CARE

Abingdon Essential Guides

Justo L. González, *Church History*
Steven M. Sheeley and Robert N. Nash, Jr., *The Bible in English Translation*
Lynn Japinga, *Feminism and Christianity*
Robin W. Lovin, *Christian Ethics*
Carlos F. Cardoza-Orlandi, *Mission*
Ronald J. Allen, *Preaching*
Jacob Neusner, *Rabbinic Literature*
Walter Brueggemann, *Worship in Ancient Israel*

PASTORAL CARE

An ESSENTIAL GUIDE

John Patton

ABINGDON PRESS
Nashville

PASTORAL CARE
AN ESSENTIAL GUIDE

Copyright © 2005 by Abingdon Press

This book is printed on acid-free paper.

Library of Congress Cataloging-in-Publication Data

Patton, John, 1930-
    Pastoral care : an essential guide / John Patton.
      p. cm.
    Includes bibliographical references.
    ISBN 0-687-05322-6 (pbk.: alk. paper)
    1. Pastoral care. I. Title.

BV4011.3.P367 2005
253—dc22

                                                            2004022200

All Scripture quotations unless noted otherwise are taken from the *New Revised Standard Version of the Bible*, copyright © 1989, by the Division of Christian Education of the National Council of the Churches of Christ in the United States of America. Used by permission. All rights reserved.

Scripture noted KJV is from the King James or Authorized Version of the Bible.

05 06 07 08 09 10 11 12 13 14—10 9 8 7 6 5 4 3 2

MANUFACTURED IN THE UNITED STATES OF AMERICA

Contents

Introduction

W hat is an essential guide for pastoral care? The word "essential" comes from the Latin word for "to be" and describes what is "basic, absolutely necessary and indispensable for carrying out a particular purpose." A "guide" is most often understood as a person or thing that conducts strangers through a region or serves as a model for conduct. "Guide" is also associated with an old English word for being wise. The meaning of these words suggests that this book is intended to provide the basic wisdom necessary to perform the ministry of pastoral care.

The ministry of pastoral care is based theologically on the Christian affirmation that God created humankind for relationship with God and with God's other creatures. God continues in relationship with humankind by remembering and hearing us. Our human caring is based in God's care; we care for each other because God cares for us. Pastoral care is the action of a community of faith that celebrates God's care by also hearing and remembering those who are in some way cut off from the faith community. What is essential for providing this caring ministry—pastoral hearing and remembering—is what this book is about.

Pastoral care within the Christian tradition is inescapably associated with the image of the shepherd. For the ordained pastor of a congregation, being a shepherd involves a tension between the responsibility for the parish or other entity, as the term "pastor in charge" suggests, and responsibility for those who are in some way separated from the others as described by the image of the lost sheep in Luke 15. The oversight function of the pastor involves teaching, preaching, organizing, and other functions that build and strengthen the whole group. The care for those in some way lost or separated from that community by choice or circumstance involves bringing the religious community and its meanings to the separated ones through the presence of a pastoral person. That person may be the pastor in charge of a particular faith community or a member of a congregation who has been recognized by that community as a lay minister of pastoral care.

It seems clear that observable success in ministry for most ordained clergy is based more on what the minister offers to the whole community for which he or she is responsible than on the care of those separated from it. The minister's effectiveness is more likely to be judged by the way he or she preaches, teaches, plans, and carries out the program of the church. This means that pastoral care for those temporarily or permanently separated from the community of faith is often an "interruptive" ministry—something that interrupts the main responsibilities that engage the pastor.

Quite often it makes little administrative sense to risk the work with "the ninety and nine" in order spend time with the one, but Luke 15 calls the pastor as shepherd to find time to care for the one that is lost, even at the risk of his or her larger responsibility for the whole group. An important part of being a pastor is balancing the work of caring for the lost sheep with the work of care for those who at least appear not to be lost. If we take seriously the caring irrationality that appears in Jesus' parable of the lost sheep, there will always be a tension between those two functions of the pastor. For the clergy for whom ministry is their calling and career, pastoral care involves the responsibility of caring for the whole community. Sometimes, however, they are called to risk their work for the community as a whole in order to reach out to the part of it that may be lost or separated.

There is something about lost sheep that calls us. The ministry of pastoral care is most often associated with that calling. The father of clinical pastoral education, Anton Boisen, believed that a major source of theological understanding lay in the experience of loneliness, particularly in the experience of those forsaken and forgotten by church and society. For Boisen, the strength of clinical education for ministry was not in its association with health care, the white coat of the hospital staff, or the psychological wisdom of the physician or psychoanalyst. It was, rather, the power of human relationship to reach out and affirm the humanness of the separated ones—those trapped in loneliness, confusion, and often, powerlessness. That is still the case. Pastors learn to deal with their own hurts and those of the community of faith by hearing and responding to the pain of those separated from that community. In order to experience their full humanness, pastors need the lost sheep as much as the lost sheep needs them.

The Twenty-third Psalm is the primary text that defines the character of the pastor as shepherd. The words "pastor" and "pastoral" are associated with the image and function of the shepherd and with representing the shepherd Lord described in the psalm. "He restores my soul." "He leads me in right paths." "I fear no evil" because the shepherd is with me. The focus of the psalm is on the presence and guidance of the Lord in restoring the soul of those in "the darkest valley." The essential ministry of those who follow that Lord is to offer presence and guidance toward the restoring of soul.

Restoring soul to those who are in some way lost or separated from the community of faith is far more than a role to play or a function to perform. It involves the wisdom to know, be, and do what is necessary to restore persons to the way that God created them. The Hebrew word for soul, *nephesh*, literally means the breath of life. It is the vitality that makes one what he or she essentially is. Theologically, a pastor is not called to care for persons by solving their problems. He or she is called to recognize and communicate, even in the most difficult circumstances, what a person really is. Care is pastoral when it looks deeper than the immediate circumstances of a person's life and reminds that person that he or she is a child of God created in and for relationship. What is essential for pastoral care is developing the theological and practical wisdom to do this.

Pastoral wisdom involves knowing, being, and doing. The order of these terms does not necessarily reflect their relative importance. No one is more important than the other two. In many cases of care, doing something or being something comes before knowing all that we need to know. Pastoral wisdom includes academic knowledge, but much of it is knowledge gained through the actual practice of ministry and reflection on that practice. Although a book can be a useful guide for this process, the best way to develop the practical knowledge of care is an ongoing educational experience that requires us to reflect on what we do, what we know, and what we are.

Clinical pastoral education is the kind of education that can do this. It is clinical in that it involves the actual practice of care and reflection on that care with a supervisor, consultant, or group of peers. It involves theories about particular types of situations, but its focus is much more on a particular pastoral event than on theories about it. It involves developing knowledge about oneself, the effect of one's presence and, in light of that, the kind of care that can be most effectively offered by a particular carer. Ideally this kind of education can be found in a program accredited by the Association for Clinical Pastoral Education, but where participation in such a program is not feasible, the necessary action-reflection process can be sought through the use of a consultant or a trusted professional colleague so that situations calling for pastoral care and their implication for one's ministry can be discussed confidentially.

Because an essential guide to pastoral care is about the development of the wisdom to offer the most effective care, the first chapter of this book is about wisdom and some of the ways that wisdom and pastoral practice are related. It is about knowing—knowing about some things that are involved in care—but it is the kind of wisdom that also includes being and doing.

Chapters 2 and 3 focus more specifically on the being and doing involved in wisdom. Following the lead of the Twenty-third Psalm, what is essential for care is presence and guidance. These are easily understood words, but what is involved in offering them is not easy. It requires wisdom to offer one's presence and guidance. At the same time discerning the meaning of presence and guidance is a means of developing pastoral wisdom about those things that are essential to pastoral care. The chapter on pastoral presence discusses what it involves, how it develops, some of its limitations, and how presence can demonstrate wisdom. The chapter on pastoral guidance discusses how this traditional aspect of pastoral work can be offered wisely through a thorough understanding of the situation of the one needing care.

Some of what needs to be known in pastoral care is practical knowledge about the dark valleys through which persons must walk in life. Certainly, there are many more of these valleys than can be discussed in this book, but those that seem most challenging to both the pastoral person and the patient or parishioner are the "dark valleys" of loss and grief, of illness, of abuse and addiction, and of family relationships. It is essential that pastors have some specific knowledge of these human problems as well as develop useful ways of addressing these situations. Thus the book has chapters that discuss each of these conditions and what may be involved in the pastoral wisdom that addresses them.

The last chapter of the book is about the more structured, though not necessarily longer term, pastoral care that is called pastoral counseling. The chapter will deal with what a pastor can do when counseling in a parish situation and with the importance and value of effective referrals to other helping persons.

In considering how to use this book, the first five chapters are appropriate for both clergy and lay carers. The last three chapters (addressing the issues of abuse and addiction, marriage and family issues, and pastoral counseling) assume the involvement of a helping person who has been invested by church and society with more authority than that given to lay carers. Those chapters, therefore, are directed primarily to the clergy and to those on a career path to become full-time ministers. It is also important to note that what is discussed about wisdom, presence, and guidance in the first three chapters is essential for the use of the material about specific pastoral concerns in the last four chapters of the book. What is essential for all pastoral care is the wisdom of knowledge, presence, and guidance to restore the soul of those for whom we care.

CHAPTER 1

Pastoral Wisdom

But where shall wisdom be found? and where is the place of understanding?
—Job 28:12 KJV

In the middle of the book of Job there is a break in the narrative. Job's plight and his friends' efforts to help him are left for a while, and instead there appears a poem about wisdom. It expresses poetically what the reader of Job already suspects—that the dialogue between Job and his friends can provide no satisfactory answer to his problem. Although some scholars have argued that this section of Job is a later addition to the narrative, others see it as integral to the book's structure. In either case, as evidenced by the ineffective efforts of Job's friends to care for him, the poem serves as a valuable reminder of the importance of developing some kind of pastoral wisdom.

Where can wisdom be found to deal with the human lostness that calls for pastoral care? Human beings can know and discover so many things in the world, but the wisdom to deal with the practical and painful situations in their own lives and in the lives of others involves a never-ending search. What kind of wisdom is essential in the care for human hurt? It certainly must include knowledge about pastoral care in general and about many of the particular situations that call for such care. Pastoral wisdom, however, includes more than knowledge about something. It involves the practical knowledge of how to do and to be. It involves being able to respond appropriately to situations calling for care, and,

7

sometimes most important, how who one is and what one represents is a part of that wisdom. Pastoral wisdom involves our knowing, being, and doing.

What Wisdom Is

Wisdom is commonly understood as the ability to make sound choices and good decisions. It is not something a person is born with. It comes from living, from making mistakes and learning from them. Wisdom is often thought of as a state of mind characterized by profound understanding and deep insight. Although it is often accompanied by intelligence and academic knowledge, that is not always necessary. In fact, wisdom can be found among relatively uneducated persons who have developed it through learning from their experience. A person who has wisdom is one who maintains a larger view of the situation to be addressed without losing sight of particularity and the intricacies of interrelationships within it. Thus wisdom involves the acceptance of complexity in a situation as matter-of-fact. This is demonstrated in the recognition that the relationships between persons and things are not always the same—that there is a messiness and disorder in life that must be dealt with.

The books of the Bible known as the Wisdom literature—Job, Proverbs, and Ecclesiastes—can be a resource for developing both personal and pastoral wisdom. Many persons have turned to these books less frequently than others because they appear to be more about human relationships than about the relationship of God and humankind. There is less talk about God in them, more language that is not specifically religious. Thus, at first glance they may seem less inspiring than other books of the Bible.

Theologically, the Wisdom literature of the Bible seems more concerned with creation than redemption. Old Testament scholar Carol Newsom describes the Wisdom literature as affirming God's creative activity by which the orderliness and dependability of the world is achieved.[1] Human wisdom is having insight into this world in order to live successfully and harmoniously. Biblical wisdom affirms the goodness of creation and believes that the good life in a material sense is not in essential conflict with the good life in the moral sense. The essence of such wisdom is to appreciate the relationship between one's acts and their consequences for oneself and for others. Wisdom is essentially concerned with the creation of a good life in the family, in the local community, and in the larger society. Pastoral care is also involved with these practical human concerns, assuming that persons' relationship with God is a part of them whether God is talked about or not.

It is the very human quality of these books, however, that offers important guidance for the ministry of pastoral care. The Wisdom literature of the Bible can remind pastors that more often than not pastoral care involves dealing with people who talk of practical, everyday problems more than they talk of God. Unlike other parts of ministry that involve teaching and preaching about God and religion, what is essential for pastoral care is familiarity and comfort with ordinary, secular language. The Bible's Wisdom literature and pastoral care are similar in their spending most of their time addressing the way things are in the world of everyday life. Wisdom in pastoral care involves learning to talk seriously about life with or without always having to talk about God.

Where Wisdom May Be Found

Knowing something about wisdom is an important part of developing it, and a book like this may serve as a guide. A more important part of developing pastoral wisdom, however, is experience in life. Wisdom for ministry begins in action, in doing ministry in the best way we know how, but developing the most effective wisdom for pastoral care requires a particular kind of experience. Just doing it is not enough to learn most effectively. The wisdom of caring emerges from bringing together three things: actually doing pastoral care; sharing what has happened in that ministry in a community of ministers; and reflecting on the meaning of those pastoral events and one's development in ministry within that community.

Two philosophers have said some things about experience that can be helpful in learning from it most effectively. The first one is Sören Kierkegaard in his criticism of philosophy's tendency to think instead of act. His concern was to move away from thinking about what we do abstractly or from a distance. He wanted to restore the involvement of the person in what he or she thought and how he or she acted. Kierkegaard spoke of the power of an individual to forge his or her personality out of the events of life. The religious self for him was not a substance or permanent presence, but an ongoing task to be achieved.[2] Similarly, becoming a wise pastor is a continuing task for the minister.

Kierkegaard said that one becomes a genuine person by what one chooses to do and to be and through risking looking at oneself and one's choices. Becoming oneself is something to be won through the experiences of life. Kierkegaard's emphasis on personal involvement and the necessity of risk in looking at oneself and what one has done is an important guide for developing pastoral wisdom. There is always the risk of exposing our failures and inadequacy in this kind of self-examination, but action and risk of the self through examining what one does in ministry is an essential part of learning to be an effective pastor.

Pastoral wisdom is developed through action and reflection on that action, but it should be a particular kind of action—action in *relationship.* A more recent philosopher, John Macmurray, can be helpful here. He was convinced that looking at the self or individual alone was a problem for philosophy and the wrong place to start in understanding life. Like Kierkegaard he was convinced that the self is first a doer and only secondarily a thinker,[3] but he emphasized the importance of relationship in the understanding of oneself and others.[4] The individual thinker tends to isolate himself or herself in the thinking process, and thus tends to see theory and practice as separated from each other. Macmurray was convinced that it is through the practical encounter in relationship that real knowledge emerges. The other person is discovered both as the resistance to, and the support of what one does. The unity of persons in community is not a fusion of self but a unity of persons where each remains a distinct individual, but each realizes himself or herself in and through the other.[5]

Kierkegaard's and Macmurray's concerns together emphasize self-reflection on action within relationship as major contributors to the development of pastoral wisdom. The action of pastoral care takes place because of the convictions and concerns of the religious community, because of the relationships within that community, and in order to strengthen those relationships with those in some way estranged from that community. Thus, relationships within a community of faith support individual action and that action contributes to enriched and strengthened relationships within and beyond the immediate community. Action in ministry grows out of one's experience in relationship and is intended to facilitate further relationship.

As has already been suggested, there are three things that contribute to the development of wisdom in pastoral care: actually doing pastoral care; sharing what has happened in that ministry in a community of ministers; and reflecting on the meaning of those pastoral events and one's development in ministry within that community of other ministers. Although philosophers Kierkegaard and Macmurray, themselves thinkers, were critical of thinking separated from action or relationship, thinking is an essential part of pastoral wisdom. The thinking or interpretation of events that is involved in the development of pastoral wisdom, however, is different from abstract thought.

One of those who underscored this truth was psychologist Paul Pruyser, who was a major contributor to modern pastoral care. Pruyser brought action, relationship, and meaning together in what he called "transformational knowledge." This knowledge, he said, comes not from abstract theories but from practical engagements intended to produce change in the person to whom help is offered and in the person offering help. In such relationships, practitioners, pastors, and others often have to make innovative decisions, not infrequently by an intuitive wisdom. Gaining transformational knowledge always involves the "messy" aspects of human life, those things that can't be theorized about or worked out beforehand. These aspects of life, however, require as much thought as the more academic or controllable dimensions of life, and this thinking is most often done after action for help or change has taken place.[6]

Bringing together the contributions of these three thinkers—Kierkegaard, Macmurray, and Pruyser—to our understanding of the wisdom required for pastoral care, we can affirm that pastoral wisdom grows out of experiencing the changing dimensions of human life through the interrelationship of action, relationship, and meaning. The best place for the interaction of these components of wisdom to take place is in a small group of colleagues in ministry where the often messy, personal, and necessarily confidential aspects of human life may be discussed freely. Talking about one's experiences in pastoral caring can simply be talking about what's happening to someone else—in effect, gossip—unless that conversation takes place in a community that has been intentionally formed to contribute to the care and the development of persons.

Pastoral reflection on action in ministry avoids objectifying others and emphasizes self-examination. It is a discussion of the pastoral self in relationship, a particular carer's action in ministry, an examination of the kind of relationship that grew out of that action, and a reflection of the meaning of that action and relationship to ministry and theology. Certainly, one can learn from one's experiences by reflecting on them alone, but the tendency there is simply to grade them as good or bad and avoid looking at the details of the situation. The observations of colleagues multiply the learning potential in a situation of ministry. Members of the group who have common commitment to ministry and openness to learning from their experience can support each other in looking realistically at what has happened and consider alternatives that are appropriate for the particular minister involved.

Although employing a consultant for a ministry group is not necessary, the wisdom that a consultant may bring is a valued addition to the group. A consultant is usually someone with more experience in ministry or more general experience in working with persons in groups. She may be a mental health practitioner, pastoral counselor, or specialist in organizational development. The consultant's value rests in her experience, knowledge of persons, groups, and leadership, and in being separate from the group of colleagues in the consultation experience. The consultant is employed to respond without any kind of personal involvement in the situation. She may know a great deal about similar situations, but unlike a supervisor who has some responsibility for what happens, the consultant can speak freely without concern for anything other than the person presenting the situation in the group.

What happens in this kind of group? A group like this is not simply involved in case studies that might be about any person or situation in general. A member of the group presents a pastoral event or situation of ministry, such as the one described in the next section. The personal involvement of the person presenting the situation is an essential element in what can take place. The group is not just discussing a particular situation as one might talk about another person's life situation. It is concerned with learning from a situation in which one of its members has been involved. The group's focus is as much (or more) on the member and his or her development in ministry as it is on the situation itself. One of the valuable contributions of a skilled consultant is maintaining this focus. Otherwise there is a natural defensiveness that causes persons to externalize the situation rather than look at themselves.

An Illustration of How Pastoral Wisdom Can Be Found

A great deal more could be said theoretically about how wisdom in pastoral care may be found. What is most important is encouraging the minister to find or organize a group in which he or she can participate. Instead of saying more in general about such groups, however, it seems more valuable now to describe an action in ministry that might be dealt within such a group. The ministry situation that is described here is far from dramatic. In fact it is quite ordinary. Nevertheless, it is just that ordinariness that can best illustrate how group consultation about everyday pastoral events can offer insight about ministry and about oneself. The pastoral event described here is not intended to illustrate what is good pastoral care, but to present the kind of situation that can have great potential for developing pastoral wisdom.

One of the members of a ministry consultation group has been to visit an older adult in his church who has been hospitalized for respiratory problems. Her only daughter lives out of town with her family and has made several unsuccessful attempts to relocate her mother to an assisted living community near where the daughter lives. The mother, however, is insistent that she will not move away from where she lives now, away from her friends and her church. The conversation that the minister presented is something like this.

13

Pastor 1: How are you feeling today?

Mrs. M 1: Well, I am fine I guess. I am just an old woman with lots of health challenges and no one to take care of me.

P2: It was really good to meet your daughter.

M2: Yes, she lives three hours away and she really wants me to move closer to her, but you know, I grew up in this church. My parents and grandparents and their parents were members at this church, and we have a long history here in this community. None of my family ever moved away from this area, and I don't plan to be the first.

P3: Did I understand you to be saying that you are presently facing many health challenges? (He goes back to pick up what he missed earlier.)

M3: Yes, I am, but "S" is my only daughter, and the reason she has gone out there is to please her husband and she needs to come back to here. Everything is here for her. I have no one else to inherit the family property and I need someone to take care of me. Can you imagine me at this stage of my life trying to do groceries? I am so grateful to some friends at church who take me to the supermarket with them every week. But I can't always depend on people. I have a daughter and she needs to help me.

P4: I am sure that your daughter must feel torn between you and her husband.

M4: Well, if she is really torn she will come back to Atlanta. I took care of her father until his dying day, and she knows how I feel about family. She knows that I never wanted her to move so far away, and yet she is out there and I am here and not able to take care of myself.

P5: Has your daughter discussed the possibility of assisted living with you?

M5: Oh yes, she has, and I will have none of it. They tell me that in those places the nurses don't take care of you like your family can. They leave you all up to your own devices and I want my daughter to be here taking care of me.

14

P6: Do you have any friends who live in an assisted living community?

M6: No. My friends have children who will take care of them and be there for them. My only daughter needs to do just that.

P7: So how do you know about the kind of care that is given in the assisted living community?

M7: Oh, I hear lots of stories.

P8: Well, I hear lots of stories too about assisted living communities, but the stories I hear are such wonderful stories of making new friends, stories about learning new hobbies, stories about eating the right kind of food, stories about taking field trips to parks and gardens—those are just some of the stories I hear. Have you ever had the chance to go visit an assisted living community?

M8: No, I have not.

P9: When you are up to it do you think that you at least would go see what one looks like? Just to visit and see what they do and how other older adults like you are living in those communities. I could talk with your daughter about it and also arrange it if you would like me to.

M9: I guess it would not hurt to go see this place, but you need to talk to my daughter and see what she thinks. I am just so tired of trying to take care of myself and my daughter is not cooperating with me. I really need the help. This last incident was a close call, and I don't think that if I were alone I would have survived. I worry about that. Talk to her and see what she says.

P10: But you are willing to go visit an assisted living community?

M10: If it's all right with my daughter, yes.

What kind of pastoral wisdom can be learned from a situation such as this one? The first thing is that the minister was willing to present it. It is an ordinary, everyday, unremarkable event, but, perhaps only because it was time for him to share himself with his group, he presented it. In doing so he was able to learn something about ministry and about his own style in pastoral care. The advantage of presenting specific, concrete events—even though they are somewhat distorted by memory—is that they bring pastoral experience back to life. Furthermore, that kind of presentation avoids the kind of distancing from one's experience that can occur when a situation is discussed only in generalities. A closer look at this pastoral encounter will reveal how much is going on in this ordinary conversation, and how it is always unfortunate to dismiss such an event with the preliminary judgment, "Not much really happened." The beginning of pastoral wisdom is noticing and describing.

In the beginning of this conversation, the parishioner answers the conventional, "How are you feeling today" with "Fine, I guess. I'm just an old woman with lots of health problems." The minister appropriately acknowledges meeting the woman's daughter for the first time, but in doing so ignores what his parishioner has said about herself. It's striking how much can be said about oneself in the two words, "I'm just. . . ." Those are words that ask the hearer to pay attention to the feeling behind them.

The parishioner uses the minister's comment about the daughter to get into the conflict between her and her daughter. He remembers that he missed the first opportunity to respond to his parishioner's health and goes back to it. This is one of the very good things about this pastoral conversation. The pastor seems to notice what he missed, goes back to it, and gives the parishioner a choice about which of the things mentioned she needs to talk about. The concern about her place in this community and the relationship with her daughter seems more pressing than her health, so that is where the conversation stays.

Although some members of the group might have raised a question with the minister about what he was feeling in the conversation before this point, at P4 either a group member or the consultant is likely to raise that question with something like this. "Did you really know what the daughter was feeling, or were you responding to something that you felt?" The minister might have acknowledged his discomfort or irritation at the church member's description of her situation and relationship to her daughter's family. His feeling might simply refer to the situation or to the parishioner herself or to something similar in his own life situa-

16

tion. Depending on their relationship to him, the group and the consultant might help him get in touch with what was going on with him as well as in the situation. There are a variety of questions that can be raised and learned from here.

In M4 the elderly parishioner continues to express her hurt and angry feelings about her daughter and her own life situation. One might suspect that she said a good deal more than the minister recorded here. The minister listens for a while, but then moves on with what seems to be his own agenda—moving away from the parishioner's feelings toward a practical solution to her problem.

This pastoral event is particularly useful in illustrating how a commonplace encounter in ministry can raise a variety of questions about how one learns and develops pastoral wisdom. What should be the focus of the consultation group's reflection on the event? The answer to that question depends both on the event and on what the group members bring to the interpretation of the event. Looking at the event from the view of what is most often helpful in pastoral care, the pastor should probably have stayed longer with the parishioner's feelings—encouraging her to express her anger, hurt, and perhaps, helplessness and hopelessness.

How the pastor offers his presence in response to another's feelings is an important part of what is presented in the next chapter. The pastor should be present with the parishioner in her painful and somewhat irrational feelings because it is unlikely that anyone else will. Learning to do this is essential to the development of pastoral wisdom.

Another useful possibility in reflecting on this event would involve focusing even more on the one who presented it. In actuality, the presenter was an international student separated geographically from his home and family. One of the concerns of the group, therefore, was the pain of the separation from his own family that might have been stirred by this event. A related question and concern might be how this parishioner is like or different from an important person in the pastor's own history. What kinds of feelings are stirred in him by this conflict between the mother or the daughter? How can he use such feelings to be present with the parishioner but not get his own concerns so involved that they seriously bias the way he responds? The group members have their own relationship to this pastor, and they may want to wonder if the way he relates to them is similar to or different from the way he responds to his parishioner.

There are many possible pastor-focused questions that can be raised in relation to a relatively simple pastoral event. They are concerned, however, not so much with finding the "right" thing to say or do in this situation as with facilitating the development in ministry of this particular pastor—increasing his practical wisdom for care.

Another possible focus in reflecting on this event is examining the way that the pastor moved in to attempt to solve the problem as he perceived it. The parishioner first rejects his attempts to suggest another way of dealing with her situation, but then seems to open up to the possibility of having someone other than her daughter care for her. Is it the pastor's calm, nonargumentative, but insistent manner of presenting his point of view that seems to make the difference? What are the most useful ways to guide persons in addressing their problems? How does the pastor avoid simply substituting himself and his authority for what the parishioner is presently dependent on? Some of these questions will be addressed in the chapter on pastoral guidance. For now, the concern is to notice the variety of perspectives that can be useful in learning from a simple pastoral event. All of them can contribute to the learning of pastoral wisdom in the interrelationship of action, relationship, and meaning that occurs in a group committed to developing in ministry.

Summary and Reflection

This chapter has addressed the question of what is essential in pastoral care through a discussion of pastoral wisdom and where it may be found. It offered some more general definitions of wisdom and then moved to a brief interpretation of the Wisdom literature of the Bible and what its view of God and the world can offer to pastoral care. God is not talked about much in the Wisdom literature. God's presence in God's world is simply taken for granted. The ordinary events of life are assumed to be related to God; therefore the wisdom writers did not have to talk about God to bring God into the situation. Pastoral care is like that. Pastoral wisdom involves the same assumption and affirms the importance of practical talk without having to talk about God in order to make the conversation have theological significance. Certainly, talk about God may be a part of the event, but that is not what makes it pastoral or theological.

From defining and describing what wisdom is, the chapter moved to the question of where wisdom can be found. It asserted that the practical wisdom of pastoral care is most effectively developed through a particular kind of learning from experience. We learn most effectively not from experience alone, but by reflecting on experience among a group of colleagues in ministry. That group reflection involves dialogue about action in ministry, relationships, and interpretation of events. None of these three important elements is satisfactory without the others. Finally, there was a presentation of an ordinary pastoral event and some of the ways that pastoral wisdom can be developed through reflecting on it.

In the next chapter we move from how pastoral wisdom may be developed to what is involved in that wisdom. As this chapter has suggested, pastoral wisdom involves a particular kind of knowledge, but it also involves two other things: our presence and guidance. The next two chapters discuss presence and guidance and will make the reader more aware that essentially pastoral care involves knowing, being, and doing.

CHAPTER 2

Pastoral Presence

I will fear no evil: for thou art with me. —Psalm 23:4 KJV

These words from the Shepherd Psalm suggest as much about the meaning of pastoral care and the development of pastoral wisdom as any in scripture. Pastoral care involves not just what you know, but also what you are. Thus, this chapter is about presence, the power of "being with" that the psalm describes. Christian faith affirms God's presence with us—God's remembering and hearing us wherever we are. The pastoral carer is a reminder of this affirmation by his remembering and hearing the person cared for.

The words "presence" and "present" come from combining "pre," which is associated in its origins with the word "pray," and "-ence" which grew out of the Latin verb to be, "esse." To pray is often understood as asking that something might happen. Thus placing "pre" or "pray" before the word for being seems to be asking for or describing being in its fullness. Because the Latin word meaning "to be," "esse," is the primary building block of the words "essence" and "essential," one's essence can be understood as being what one was meant to be. Theologically, this has been understood as being in touch with God.

The concern here is not with word origins as such, but with what they suggest about the meaning of presence in pastoral care. If "pre" is a form of "pray," and "-ence" a form of "essence" or

21

"being," pastoral care must certainly involve praying to be or to become one's essential self. That could mean a number of things. It might mean praying to be my best self or praying to be aware of my connection or relationship to God. It could mean the risk of changing my comfortable or familiar self in response to a difficult or challenging situation. My presence involves my awareness of my "esse," or being, and my awareness of the "being" of those to whom I offer care. "Presence" is a heavily loaded word, and being in touch with its meaning can enrich our experience and understanding of pastoral care.

The pastoral carer, whether laity or clergy, is present to the person cared for in a particular kind of relationship—one that "re-presents" the presence of God through relationship to the person cared for. Pastoral carers "re-present" or remind persons of God by remembering and hearing, and affirm by their action that God continues to hear and remember them.

God is "re-presented" in relationship most effectively—there is genuine pastoral presence in the relationship—when (1) the carer's own person is fully present and he is aware of himself and his own feelings; (2) when the carer is fully aware that he represents more than himself; and (3) when he is aware of and able to experience as much as possible the unique personhood of the one to whom care is offered. All three of these dimensions of presence involve awareness—developing awareness of self, of what one represents, and increasing awareness of the personhood of those cared for.

Presence in the Person of the Carer

Although the ministry of pastoral care involves knowing something and doing something, it is most of all about being something. It is not just about reaching out to the person cared for. It is about oneself. It order to be present, to "be with," the carer's being or full selfhood must be there. The carer is one who is seeking to be more than he is. The church has always expected this from its ministers. The question about this does not have to be as radical as the historic Methodist question about its ministers at annual conferences: "Are all ministers blameless in life and character?"

22

Nevertheless, the question reminds us that the kind of person a minister is, whether laity or clergy, is important.

The meaning of the word "character" grows out of the term's use in printing, where a character is a distinctive mark, such as a letter or a symbol. Character applied to a person is similarly understood as a distinctive mark, a distinctive trait, quality or attribute, an essential quality. Secondarily, character has meant moral strength, self-discipline, or fortitude. It has also meant having a definable role, such as a character in a play. All of these meanings are associated with the person of the pastoral carer.

David Duncombe has identified six dimensions of spiritual or religious life in the Christian tradition that have been used to describe the distinctive mark of the minister.[1] All six reflect the difficulty of identifying Christian character with any single thing. Thus there are contrasting meanings or two sides for each of the dimensions of character. The character of the minister should be both:

1. *Mystical and moral.* The first side suggests some kind of union with God and the second reminds us of social obligations to humankind.

2. *Sacred and secular.* One side represents the encounter with God at special times and places, such as in worship. The other side affirms the possibility of divine presence at all times and in all places.

3. *Individual and corporate.* This dimension emphasizes the minister's individual religious quest, and the importance of membership in the gathered community.

4. *Belief and faith.* Belief takes seriously the historical convictions of the faith community, while faith emphasizes the creative and new insights that appear to be relatively unrelated to a particular set of beliefs.

5. *Virtue and ability.* One side emphasizes particular Christian virtues as necessary for Christian life and ministry—for example, the Galatians 5:22 list which includes love, joy, peace, and so on—and the other side emphasizes that any ability can express the Christian life and ministry if it is rooted in God.

6. *Perfection and wholeness.* The striving for perfection, as commended by Christ in Matthew 5:48, is on one side, and on the other side is a wholeness emphasizing balance or integration of the good and bad which is present in all human beings.

The richness of these dimensions reveals the complexity of describing what the person of the minister, the pastoral carer, ought to be. What is most important is not some strict compliance with one or both sides of these dimensions, but that their representation of what the minister "ought to be" is taken seriously. Reflecting prayerfully on what these dimensions of character might mean in his or her life can guide the minister in becoming a pastoral presence.

Presence in the Awareness of the Carer

It may seem paradoxical, but full awareness of and care for the other require full awareness of oneself and what one is experiencing. This book is about pastoral wisdom, and an essential part of pastoral wisdom is wisdom about what one is feeling and experiencing in the pastoral relationship.

The immense value of a consultation group on ministry in which one can be honest about the pastoral events that occur in one's ministry is that such a group can increase one's self-awareness. Other group members notice things about you and what you may have been feeling that you yourself have not noticed. Group members (and preferably a skilled consultant meeting with the group) notice and share with the carer both strengths and weaknesses that he or she may have been unaware of. Reflecting in community about one's self-awareness in ministry is an essential element in the development of the kind of presence involved in pastoral wisdom.

The carer needs to become aware of how what has happened in his or her life may be affecting what he or she hears and responds to. A recent loss of a loved one by the carer may significantly affect what and how he or she hears and responds to the losses in another's life. She may be tempted to talk about her own loss, or, on the other hand, may steer the other person away from talking about any sadness at all. What is important, both prior to entering a relationship and in later reflections about it, is being aware of how one's own life experience may affect response to another's life. That awareness may involve that carer's knowledge that she is at a point in life when she herself is in need of care and that need is affecting her care of others.

Awareness of oneself and what is going on in one's experience is an essential part of the presence required in pastoral care. Another essential is an ongoing development of oneself in the Christian life. One might call this the spiritual and intellectual preparation for being a pastor. This is something that is important for both laity and clergy. Ordained ministers have completed the required academic preparation required by their denomination for ordination. Lay ministers have been trained and certified in some way, but for both kinds of ministers, a study and search of their faith and tradition is required. One could call this spiritual preparation for ministry or a quest to become more "faith-full." It can take place in a variety of ways, both individually and in community. The important thing for one's being and one's presence in pastoral care is that it is something going on now.

Presence Through What the Carer Represents

God is "re-presented" in a pastoral relationship when the carer is aware that he represents more than himself and more than his particular community of faith. The presence he offers is more than his presence. He is a reminder and re-presenter of God, faith, the church, and all that religion may represent to the person cared for. It is important that the carer be aware that he is not the one who "brings God" into the room of the person cared for. The faith that he represents affirms that God has been there and is there now. The carer is a part of bringing that presence into some kind of awareness in the person cared for and in himself.

What is involved in a pastoral relationship has most often been discussed in terms of the role, function, and identity of a minister. A role is an external perception of what one is and how one functions in relation to a particular society or community. It is the way in which the individual in his ordinary work situations presents

25

himself to others, the ways in which he guides and controls the impressions they form of him, and the kinds of things he may and may not do while performing in his role. Carrying out a role always involves visibility and function. Visibility emphasizes the power of the role itself, however actively one accepts or "plays" it. Function underscores the importance of action in carrying out the role, however effective or ineffective that action may be. Thus it is essential for a minister to be seen as minister by both church and community and to have the function of minister for those who view him in that way.

How one is visible in a pastoral role is always a central issue in learning pastoral care. In her supervised ministry in a hospital, for example, the theological student or lay minister may feel that she is not really a chaplain and may have difficulty in introducing herself as such. In her training, however, she is reminded by those supervising her that she has no "license" to be in the hospital except as a representative of the chaplain's department and that she must have visibility as such. Learning to be a pastor involves learning to accept and deal with what that role represents.

Even ministers who seem to be saying openly, "I accept the fact that I am minister and am proud of that fact" may have difficulty accepting all the expectations, hopes, and anger that the ministerial role can bring with it. Other people's perceptions and assumptions inevitably bring the "visible minister" to the point of saying openly to himself or herself, "But I'm not that kind of minister." It's embarrassing to be thought of as "that kind of minister." In being seen as ministers, both lay and clergy pastoral carers are identified with all the distortions and pettiness of church and ministry as well as with its greatness. And the inner dialogue that takes place as a result of the way that the minister is perceived is a significant part of developing pastoral identity.

Identity has been defined as the very "core" of a person toward which everything else is ordered. It is something that, if one knows it, provides the "clue" to a person. Identity is the specific uniqueness of a person, what really counts about him, quite apart from both comparison and contrast to others.

Pastoral identity involves the confidence that in the midst of changing circumstances I *am* a pastor and that in many ways I can take this for granted. To myself I *feel* like a pastor and, therefore, do not have to be concerned about this when I attempt to offer ministry to another person. Because pastoral identity is only a part of my total identity and is one of the later developing parts, it is more vulnerable to identity diffusion as a result of changes in role and function. As a later developing part of my identity and because it makes up only a portion of who l am, it may sometimes be competitive with earlier ways in which I thought of myself.

It is important to note that pastoral identity—identification of oneself as a minister—is an issue for both lay ministers, who function in a specialized pastoral care ministry, and for ordained clergy, who carry out all of the functions of ministry. For lay ministers who have previously had a different relationship to the persons for who they have been assigned to offer pastoral care, being seen as a minister and experiencing oneself as a minister is a somewhat surprising experience.

For example, Sarah is a lay minister who has been in a ten-week lay ministry training course provided by the nearby hospital's clinical pastoral education supervisors. She has been commissioned by her church as a lay minister and has functioned in that role a little less than a year. She is visiting a family that she has known for many years in an extended care facility. When she arrives where the patient and family are, she is introduced to a friend of this family, whom she did not previously know, as one of their church's lay ministers. In her reflection on the visit she noted that even though she had been known longer as this family's friend, in this visit they identified her as a minister of their church. Having been identified in this way during the visit, she was approached by a second friend as she was leaving the facility. This person had seen her visiting the family, and she sought Sarah's guidance about her own relationship to the family.

Later, when the consultation group for lay ministers in her church discussed this visit, much of the discussion centered around Sarah's different relationship to this family in how they perceived her, how she functioned, and how she experienced herself as a minister. Most important was Sarah's developing awareness that there was something different in her and in her relationships when she was functioning as a lay minister. She was seen differently—as more than "just Sarah." She experienced herself differently, as if something was there that was not there before, and that affected the way she functioned. She acted differently in relation to those who saw her as minister. She was freer to do things that she was less comfortable with before and, perhaps, she was less free at the same time.

This increasing awareness in Sarah of the "more" involved in her relationships when she was functioning as a minister touches on the responsibility and accountability involved in acting, being, and functioning as a minister and "re-presenter" and reminder of God. There are more things to be "care-full" with. In the role and function of minister she is not just herself. She is representing God and all things associated with God in the experience of the persons to whom she offers care. The "more" that she carries with her in being a minister allows persons to be more personal, more serious, more themselves with her than they might be otherwise in a friendship. Because that kind of intimacy is possible, however, there is always at least an implicit expectation that any intimacy present will be kept within the pastoral relationship and not carried over into a friendship.

Because she was perceived as minister, Sarah carried with her a kind of authority or power that Sarah as Sarah did not have. Her responsibility to her ministerial calling and to her colleagues in ministry require her to use this authority and power responsibly, not attributing it to her intelligence, personal charm, or other elements in her personality. The responsibility requires her to limit that authority to her pastoral function and not extend it into other relationships with that person. She may know that person well as pastor, but she may not use that knowledge for her own satisfaction in any other kind of relationship. Responsible limits on the pastoral relationship will be discussed again later in the book. Failure to recognize these limits is the cause of destructive and abusive relationships that have grown out of failure to have appropriate boundaries between the pastoral and the personal.

Presence in the Carer's Response to the Person Cared For

The first two dimensions of pastoral presence are the person of the carer and the "more than the person himself or herself" that the carer represents. The third dimension of presence is in the response that the carer offers to the person or persons for whom she cares. The carer is present by the way she responds to other. That response can be described most usefully in terms of listening: how one listens and what one listens for. Listening as we will discuss it here is not just a matter of using one's ears and hearing words. It is a total response to the way that the carer is experiencing the other.

A useful reminder of this can be found in the Synoptic Gospels. The first three Gospels consistently emphasize the importance of listening and getting the message. The contrast these Gospels make between those who hear and those who do not offers a powerful challenge for the pastoral carer. A particularly helpful example is found in Luke 8:18, which the *New Revised Standard Version* translates as "pay attention to how you listen." The Greek word literally means "see" how you listen. It denotes sense perception or being able to see as distinct from blindness, and it calls for all the senses to be used for full awareness of the message being conveyed. This text challenges the pastoral carer to be "care-full" in the way that she listens and remembers what she hears.

Just as "seeing how we listen" involves bringing together two senses, sight and hearing, how we listen needs to involve at least two things. Pastoral presence—being with this person where he is—requires, first of all, listening carefully to whatever the patient or parishioner tells the pastor about his present situation, the condition of his illness, his family, loss of a job or significant person in his life. The pastor listens to understand as much as he can about the immediate challenge to this person's life. One might think of this as the up close view of the person's present life.

Pastoral presence also requires a second type of listening, usually a somewhat more active one that attempts to place the present situation within the context of the person's whole life. The pastor can be most helpful when he or she goes into a pastoral visit with the assumption that the patient or parishioner has the task of putting the immediate crisis within the picture of his whole life. What does this illness or loss mean for what happens in the rest of his life? The patient may be looking for a specific religious meaning or he may not. Implicit in the situation, however, is the question, "where do we go from here?" This may be a very practical or a very philosophical question. It may be both. The pastor's task is to listen for it in the midst of all that is discussed in the pastoral call and to consider whether or not this is the best time for the pastor to raise the larger question of what this situation may mean for this person's life.

More will be said about this in the chapter on guidance. Here the emphasis is on what might be called "bifocal listening"—attending to the immediate situation, but listening for the opportunity to consider larger issues in the patient or parishioner's life. As has been stated and will be affirmed a number of times in this book, a pastor is not called to care for persons by solving their problems. He or she is called to recognize and communicate, even in the most difficult circumstances, that a person is more than the problem he presents. He or she is not just a medical or psychological diagnosis, a couple struggling to stay in a painful marriage, a lonely or demoralized person.

Those for whom the pastor cares are persons created for relationship with God and God's creation. The pastor may contribute the solution of the person's problem, but the pastoral care offered is not the guidance given but the relationship provided and the restoring of soul that can result from that. Rediscovering one's self and one's power to live and to change in the context of relationship is what pastoral care is all about. Care is pastoral when it looks deeper than the immediate circumstances of a person's life and reminds that person that he or she is a child of God created in and for relationship.

Pastoral presence is expressed through this kind of bifocal listening, but there is another way as well. One can make a strong case that the Bible speaks about God and also about the human situation in more than one way. There is a strong voice and a quiet voice—a majority message and a voice from the minority as well. Old Testament theologian Walter Brueggemann has argued that the Bible is filled both with testimony and countertestimony—a voice of faith and a voice that challenges that faith.[2] There is a voice that speaks in theological language and one that is presented in the more secular voice of practical ethics, such as in the book of Proverbs. There is a countertestimony in the challenging, questioning voice of Job and in the skeptical, often cynical voice of the writer of Ecclesiastes. In the psalms there are strong expressions of both testimony and countertestimony—words of faith and those of anger, pain, and doubt. The voices in the New Testament are more unified in their testimony to Jesus as the Christ, but even here there is sometimes a minority voice of questioning and doubt. It may be heard in the doubt of the disciple Thomas, or in the not-knowing voice that one sees occasionally in the apostle Paul when even this man of faith wonders "who has known the mind of the Lord?"

Pastoral presence requires hearing both the majority and minority voices from Scripture and from the persons to whom we offer care. Much of our wisdom in pastoral caring lies in hearing and responding not just to the language of faith and the church but to the secular and negative languages of grief, illness, addiction, and broken relationships. More will be said later about response to these specific challenges. The assertion here is simply that pastoral wisdom requires being present with both the positive and negative, the religious voice and the more secular voice. Although what the pastor represents is the language of faith and the church, in the ministry of pastoral care she is called to listen even more carefully to the countertestimony to faith, the negative, uncertain, doubtful voice.

Pastoral presence requires listening more carefully to that doubtful and uncertain voice because it is more difficult and more painful to hear. The scriptural text for doing this can be found in the sixth chapter of the book of Job in which Job rejects the quick answers to his problems that are proposed by his friends. He accuses them of betraying them and says plainly in verse 6:21: "You see my calamity, and are afraid." Most of those to whom the pastor ministers do not speak as clearly and assertively as did Job, but his words are a valuable reminder that the situation of those for whom we are called to care can stir our anxiety and remind us of our own vulnerability. One of the challenges of pastoral presence is to listen for and hear the countertestimony as well as the testimony of persons' lives.

Summary and Reflection

Again, pastoral presence requires one to listen bifocally in two different ways. (1) One listens to the immediate problem and to how that problem is related to the parishioner's larger story of life. (2) One listens for the testimony and the countertestimony that appear in the way a person presents his or her problems and life.

There is a final element in offering presence that complements this bifocal listening. It is a willingness to hear the way a person expresses his or her life without rushing in too quickly to diagnose and solve the problem. Again, the book of Job is helpful here. Although Job hardly seems to offer anything quickly, what one can see in that book is Job's friends offering solutions or diagnoses of his problem without first offering their presence. As the Job 6:21 text suggests they seem uncomfortable with the situation and fail to respond to the depth of what they are experiencing. Instead they try to solve it or explain it. The pastoral guidance discussed in the next chapter can only be offered if pastoral presence is experienced first.

One of the things that appears again and again in the write-ups of pastoral events by lay ministers and inexperienced pastors is how quickly they seem to move toward solving what they experience as the patient or parishioner's problem. In the pastoral event described in the previous chapter, for example, the pastor appears uncomfortable with the parishioner's somewhat irrational complaints about her daughter's failure to take care of her and moves away from her feelings to bring up an assisted care facility as a solution to the problem. Guidance of that sort may ultimately be valuable, but pastoral presence suggests that the pastor may need to deal with his own feelings of irritation with her and try to be more present with her before his specific guidance can be accepted by her.

The pastor's calling is to be present with a person in whatever lostness is a part of his or her life and to strengthen the relationship of that person to the faith community that the pastor represents. Because pastoral care is the care of the whole person in relationship, concern with specific problems is never completely separated from the broader issue of what a particular problem means for a person's life. Many persons today do not know how to address their need for relationship and care without the excuse of having a particular problem. Their problem may be the only avenue that they have for developing a relationship to a helping person that can allow them to talk with the pastoral carer about the deeper concerns of their lives. Pastoral presence certainly contributes to reducing persons' anxiety about a variety of specific concerns, but the pastor can easily get caught up in the thought that his or her relevance as a carer depends on problem solving rather than relationship. Actually, help toward solving particular problems takes place most effectively in a relational context of care when the pastor is armed with the aphorism that "Life is not a problem to be solved, but a mystery to be lived."

The chapter has discussed presence as an essential dimension of pastoral wisdom. Presence involves the person of the pastor with all of his or her self-awareness, responsible understanding and use of what the pastor represents, and response to the cared-for one that listens deeply and remembers. More will be said in the next chapter about how presence is involved in and affects pastoral guidance.

CHAPTER 3

Pastoral Guidance

He leadeth me beside the still waters. He restoreth my soul.
—Psalm 23:2-3 KJV

astoral wisdom involves knowing, being, and doing. This chapter is about guidance in pastoral care—a kind of doing that is strongly affected by what the pastor knows and what she is—her presence. Although many of the elements in presence and guidance are similar and interrelated, the chapter on presence was placed before the chapter on guidance because the distinctive feature of pastoral guidance is that it cannot take place without presence. Presence is not only prior to guidance, but also it continues on through any guidance that takes place.

Pastoral guidance includes the same three elements described in the discussion of presence: the personal involvement of the pastor with all of his or her awareness of self and other; responsible use of the pastor's role, function, and identity as a representative of God and the religious community; and the pastor's presence communicated by the way she responds to the presence of the one cared for. These three elements make appropriate pastoral guidance possible.

The word "guidance" is strongly associated with wisdom. It is derived from an earlier word that means to "observe" and with the old English word for wisdom. Guidance is also associated with leading. A guide is one who points out the way, who directs others on a course. Leading, in its origin, is understood as going before and going with, in some fashion showing the way. It is related to the word "load," suggesting that the leader is one who carries the load of responsibility for the task at hand.

All of these things about the origin of the word "guidance" are relevant to the view of pastoral guidance presented here, but what is said in this chapter about pastoral guidance is quite different from the way that the word is most often used. Guidance is most often understood as advice given by one person about what another person should do. *Pastoral* guidance is significantly different from that. It is more related to the presence of the guide and the relationship he or she offers than to a course of action suggested. Moreover, guidance as discussed here is guidance offered to a particular person or a group smaller than the whole for whom the pastor is responsible. It is quite different from what might be offered generally to a larger group in a sermon or lecture.

This book itself is an example of the more general type of guidance. It discusses what is essential in pastoral care and provides information and practical suggestions that can be useful to a wide variety of persons—clergy and laity—who are involved in the process of care. The book, in offering guidance in this general way, is neither pastoral care nor pastoral guidance. It is *about* pastoral care. The guidance that is pastoral care is not guidance relevant for all or most people, but something that may indeed be very relevant and useful to a particular person or small group.

To use the images of the care of the flock and care for the lost sheep, the guidance necessary for the whole flock is seldom the guidance that is most helpful for lost or separated sheep. One can see this in the ineffectiveness of the analysis and advice given to Job by his friends. Although pastoral guidance may include information that can be helpful to more than this particular one, it is seldom the application of what has appeared to be helpful to the many to the predicament of the one. Rather, guidance that is genuinely pastoral is something that is developed out of in-depth understanding of the predicament of this particular person separated by his present circumstances from the larger group. The pastor should measure her use of any knowledge she feels may contribute to guiding another with the awareness that it is the patient or parishioner who knows the most about the kind of guidance that he needs.

36

The most ineffective guidance a pastor can offer is a kind of generalized reassurance. The most common example is offering some version of "Everything is going to be all right." That message may indeed be true, but very seldom does the pastor know that, and the parishioner knows that he or she doesn't know that. This kind of generalized reassurance simply serves to deal with the pastor's own anxiety in not quite knowing what to say or do. The only kind of reassurance that can be effective pastoral guidance is based on specific events or behavioral changes that the pastor has noticed and the parishioner can confirm.

Guiding, as Seward Hiltner suggested some years ago, involves the tender, solicitous care involved in all genuinely pastoral work.[1] In guiding, however, the major task is not directing the person's life but *reminding* the person cared for of specific resources that have been part of his life, though they are now absent or weak. Guiding involves listening for the whole story, telling the person something of what has been heard, and reminding him that the illness, the grief, the broken relationship he is experiencing is not all that he is.

Guiding may include instruction and information, but it is aimed much less at acquiring than restoring—restoring the parishioner's soul, thus becoming more of his true self again. The images of the shepherd's guidance in the Twenty-third Psalm—still waters and right paths—contribute significantly to our understanding of the type of guidance that can be most helpful to those separated by situation or circumstance from the community of faith and their normal way of life. The Twenty-third Psalm is a comfort, but it is also a challenge to the pastor to discover and rediscover the wisdom involved in true guidance.

Leading Beside Still Waters

Pastoral wisdom is expressed first of all through the pastoral carer's ability to lead "beside still waters" or, in effect, to provide a steady and secure relationship that is relatively free from anxiety. Anxiety as it is usually experienced has been defined as a state of being uneasy, apprehensive, or worried about what may happen—concern about a possible future event. In its more extreme forms it is characterized by a feeling of being powerless and unable to cope with threatening events, typically imaginary, and by physical tension, sweating, or trembling.

Anxiety is familiar to all of us. It is usually experienced to some degree in any new or unfamiliar situation. In ministry the pastoral carer's task involves dealing with both his or her own anxiety and that of the patient or parishioner. Learning to deal with one's own anxiety in pastoral situations comes first of all through experience. Virtually all pastors get over the anxiety of new experiences and discover on reflection that the pastoral event did not go as badly as anticipated. A classic example of this anxiety can be seen in the early pages of *Leaves from the Notebook of a Tamed Cynic* where even the great American theologian Reinhold Niebuhr shares his experience of being anxious in making calls on parishioners in his first parish. "Usually I walk past a house two or three times before I summon the courage to go in. I am always very courteously received, so I don't know exactly why I should not be able to overcome this curious timidity."[2]

Clinical pastoral education and other experiences of supervised ministry have provided opportunities to beginning pastoral carers, both laity and clergy, for getting pastoral experience, sharing their anxiety, and learning from it. Experience alone helps, but when that experience can be shared with colleagues who are in a similar situation it is much more effective in reducing anxiety. Without the opportunity to share one's anxiety with a trusted friend or colleague, inappropriate degrees of anxiety are much more likely to appear at inopportune times and interfere with the pastoral relationship. The pastor's anxiety needs to be experienced, recognized, shared, and learned from, not denied. Gradually discovering what kind of situations cause the most anxiety can assist the carer in preparing for them and experiencing them as less threatening. As in any new and important situation, a prayer for calmness and a sense of direction for one's ministry is always appropriate.

Recognizing the fact of the pastoral carer's own anxiety and taking steps to address it—finding his own "still waters"—is essential for his dealing with the anxiety of the patient or parishioner. The pastor's own stillness and calmness can contribute to the parishioner's finding hers. The most frequent complaint heard about hospital visitors is that their hyperactivity, lack of calmness, too much talk, or other evidences of anxiety disturbed the patient or staff. This can be true in a home visit as well as a hospital one.

Leading a parishioner, who is in some way lost or in crisis, by still waters involves first of all assuming that the person has some anxiety about his present situation. Both theological and psychological theorists have understood anxiety as one of the major features of the human condition. In virtually every relationship there can be some anxiety about how the encounter with the other will turn out or how each will be perceived. In most any situation of personal crisis one can assume that anxiety is present. The only question is about the degree or intensity of anxiety.

Many of us have had the experience of holding a small child that has been frightened or hurt. When the child is held firmly, but gently, in the comfort of one's lap and is told very simply what has happened and or what will happen, he will usually begin to relax and be less fearful about what has or will happen. Most often nothing has changed in the threatening situation, but the firm and steady holding has led the child by "still waters," and whatever needs to take place can take place without major incident.

The pastoral care of an adult in crisis does not involve physical holding. Physical comfort is absent or minimal, perhaps expressed by a firm touch on the hand or shoulder. The holding that occurred with the child is symbolically expressed in a calm, steady presence and a few words that acknowledge the difficulty of the situation. The pastor's leading by "still waters" involves standing by and guiding through exhibiting calmness in an atmosphere that is far from calm.

In addition to this symbolic holding, the pastor offers the guidance of a secure and dependable relationship by acknowledging the parishioner's anxiety and responding to it. His or her concern is not to emphasize the anxiety, but simply to acknowledge and not ignore it. In acknowledging it, the pastor might or might not use the word "anxiety." He or she might say something like, "The uncertainty about just what is coming next (or whatever the threat seems to be) seems pretty scary. Trying to be calm is not easy." In acknowledging anxiety it is best for both pastor and parishioner to speak of it. Simply ventilating ones fears may increase them. A dialogue about them by two persons in a secure relationship tends to reduce them. The important part about this kind of guidance is that it expresses the presence of the pastor in the midst of the anxiety.

It is important to recognize that a secure relationship, one that can lead by still waters, is one that has clear boundaries and limits. The pastor guides by being present, but there are limits on his or her physical presence that allow for the symbolic presence of the caring community to be there in its stead. As suggested earlier, there should be limits on physical touching, but there should also be limits on the time a pastor spends with a particular person or family. Although there are no rigid rules for this and a pastoral relationship has many of the personal elements of friendship, there should be clear limits of time spent and personal involvement allowed by one who is functioning primarily as a pastor. There are times in crisis when a pastor may appropriately spend all night at the hospital with a patient's family, but unlimited time spent is more the function of friends and family than of the pastor. The parishioner can only be free to share her deepest concerns when she knows that there are boundaries and limits on her relationship to the pastor.

In a more structured pastoral counseling situation it is particularly important to have limits on the time to be spent in a particular session. There are a few emergency situations when the usual rules of procedure are broken—for example, threats of suicide or violence—but in most situations the pastor leads by still waters by symbolically conveying the message that "there are ways of dealing with this, and this is my usual procedure of doing so." Setting limits of time can convey the very useful message that "We'll deal with as much as we can in the time we have and then go on with the rest of our lives. This situation or problem is not the only thing in your life and mine."

Just as a parent's being away from the child can teach the child to hold on to the parent's presence when they are separated, the pastor's limits on time spent with a parishioner also conveys an important message. "You can be strengthened by relationship with me and through me with the community of faith, but you can use this relationship without constant physical presence." A similar message is conveyed by Jesus to the disciples in the Gospel of

John. "I have said these things to you while I am still with you. But the Advocate, the Holy Spirit, whom the Father will send in my name, will teach you everything, and remind you of all that I have said to you" (John 14:25-26). Although the presence of the pastoral carer is certainly not the same as the presence of Jesus, because the carer represents Christ and his church, the carer also conveys the message, "You do not need my constant physical presence because the Holy Spirit can be with you."

Finally, one of the most important boundaries involved in providing a secure relationship is the boundary that the pastor keeps between her life situation and that of the patient or parishioner. It is difficult for a patient or parishioner to trust a relationship when it seems that the pastor is working on her own life situation as well as responding to that of the parishioner. A pastor's affective response, her feelings, are the most valuable asset she has in expressing her care. Her own past experience and feelings related to that experience help her to understand and express her care for others. In tension with this, however, is the fact that those same feelings can get in the way of her responsiveness to the person cared for.

If a person is sad or depressed, the pastor's own experience of sadness can help her understand the patient or parishioner's experience, but if she gets too deeply into her own experience she may be unable to respond to the other person. The pastor may have had an experience of illness or other life-changing experience that is similar to that of her parishioner. Having a similar experience can help her understand and be responsive in the pastoral situation, but it may also tempt her to talk about her experience more than to listen to the experience of the other person. There needs to be definable limits on the pastor's self-expression of the feelings and experiences that can help her respond helpfully to another.

Most pastors need some kind of consultation with a colleague or experienced professional to help them deal with limiting self-expression. A guideline that can be used without consultation is asking oneself, when in the pastoral situation, "How much do I want to share this experience of mine with this parishioner?" If the answer comes back, "I really want or need to do it," then the experience should usually not be shared. The intensity of the desire to share indicates that the pastor is responding more to her need than to the situation of the other person. This is an important limit that allows the other to find the still waters that he needs rather than to compare his needs to the pastor's. The pastor guides by providing a secure relationship in which excessive anxiety can be reduced and the soul can be restored.

Leading into Right Paths

How does the pastor guide by leading into right paths? The answer is that in pastoral care, one offers guidance and right direction first of all by listening. The guidance that the minister offers to the whole congregation or to the larger group for which he is responsible comes from a variety of sources, theological and secular, from the Bible and the daily newspaper and so on. He attempts to offer a wisdom that has relevance for most of those to whom he teaches, preaches, and with whom he works in programs of ministry. In pastoral care he is working with severe limits on use of the wisdom and guidance that may be helpful to many. His task is to help find the right path for one or a small group that is in some way lost. The wisdom for doing that comes from listening and from being more aware of what the pastor doesn't know than what he does know.

Recall the things about guiding that were said earlier in this chapter. Guiding is not directing the person's life but *reminding* the person cared for of specific resources that have been part of his life, though they may now be absent or weak. Guiding involves listening for the whole story and reminding the person of what has been heard—reminding him that the illness, the grief, the broken relationship is not all that he is. Guiding may include instruction and information, but it is aimed less at acquiring new information than recovering old resources. In order to do this a pastor must learn how to listen and continue to improve his ability to listen throughout his ministry.

A major characteristic of guidance that is pastoral, as well as a characteristic of pastoral presence, is "care-full" listening—listening that conveys care. Characteristics of that kind of listening noted in the previous chapter were its attention to the immediate situation and to the larger picture of a person's life. Also emphasized

42

was the need to listen for the testimony and the countertestimony—the positive and negative voice in the parishioner's story. The listening necessary for pastoral guidance adds to this by bringing in the image of a life journey. The discussion was about *what* to listen for. The discussion here of listening as necessary for guidance emphasizes *how* to listen in order to guide a person on their way.

In the mid-twentieth century, the work of Carl Rogers was a powerful influence on pastoral care. What Rogers taught most effectively was the ability to listen and to convey to the other the fact that he had accurately heard. Accuracy in hearing and in conveying what has been heard is the essence of what Rogers and his colleagues taught. The carer leaves the person alone and out of relationship if the pastor is not able to listen, to hear, to respond exactly, and to help the person share what is felt. Eugene Gendlin, one of Rogers's colleagues, vividly described what happens when listening fails or, in the terms expressed here, is not "care-full."

> What the person is really up against is not dealt with, is not even brought in, is not even touched. Without listening, the inward sense of the person is not expanded, it remains not only alone, but compressed, sometimes nearly silent, dumb. That way there can be no relationship. . . . Responding in a listening way is a baseline prerequisite for any other modes of responding. It is not just one of many ways, but a precondition for the other ways. [3]

There may be types of guidance that can take place without "care-full" listening, but genuinely pastoral guidance requires it.

Just as directions to a particular geographical place are seldom useful if the starting place is not clear, the pastor needs to know as much as possible about where a particular person is in order to offer appropriate and useful guidance. The parishioner may need pastoral guidance because of illness, grief, or other kinds of "lostness." The pastor asks, "How is today going for you?" and listens in the parishioner's answer for how she is experiencing her particular type of separation from her usual life experience. He does not need to know any more of the details of her situation than the parishioner wishes to tell. Objective or external knowledge of what has happened to her is not nearly as important as how the parishioner shares her experience of it—where she is—with the pastor. The pastor listens and notices the way that she tells where she is. He then responds with some words that tell the parishioner what he has heard and that he is giving full attention to trying to understand her situation. His guidance begins to take place in the way he encourages her to tell her story.

The most helpful sequence in the guidance through listening is beginning with the present, the now, of the parishioner's situation. "What is it like for you today?" He listens for her feelings about conditions now, and then—still listening as much for feelings as for facts—he encourages the parishioner to share as much as she wants to about what led up to this. As the dialogue seems to move toward a conclusion, the pastor responds to what the parishioner seems to be hoping for or raises a question about what she hopes for. "Then what you are most hoping for after all that you have been through is . . . ?" The pastoral conversation has moved from present experience to what in the past led up to it and to the kind of hopes that the parishioner has in the light of all that has happened.

Certainly, not all pastoral conversations move in this way. Many times the immediate experience is so powerful that the patient cannot get beyond it. Sometimes she may choose not to talk about what seems to have contributed to the situation. Sometimes the pastoral carer's anxiety may prevent him from using the present, past, future sequence in this kind of guided conversation. Nevertheless, having such a sequence in mind can help both pastor and parishioner give and receive the guidance needed in moving through the terrain of a particular crisis.

What is most characteristic of this kind of guidance is the pastor's deep concern to help the parishioner identify where she is, where she has been, and where she wants to go. The pastor may know something about similar situations, but using any of this knowledge for guidance until he has become familiar with the parishioner's journey is seldom useful and reduces the ongoing sense of the pastor's presence. The kind of listening and responding that the pastor is offering might appropriately be called dialogical. It is listening that does not leave the patient or parishioner alone, but conveys the message, "I am doing the best that I can to understand where you are, and I will let you know what I am hearing and understanding." Recall the caution from the chapter on presence about too quickly jumping to conclusions about what is wrong or what needs to be done before being fully present in what is happening now. Assisting someone on a journey requires knowing the starting point as well as the prior stops along the way.

Pastoral guidance, leading in right paths, involves touching as many pieces of a person's life as that person is willing and able to share. Guiding requires general knowledge about life and how it can be lived effectively, but pastoral guidance requires knowledge of this particular life and the story that is being lived. Pastoral care, as many have said, involves the skill of listening for stories, particularly those stories that have formed the style of this person's life. These stories are most often culturally defined and require the pastor to recognize and acknowledge her limits in understanding.

Another element important in the listening necessary for pastoral guidance is the pastor's sensitivity to the developing relationship between herself and the patient or parishioner. What was the nature of the relationship before this particular pastoral event began? How is the conversation developing and what feelings of trust or distrust are evident? How comfortable is the pastor and how comfortable does the patient or parishioner seem to be? Something about the character of the relationship can be seen in the way that the parishioner shares the story of his immediate and his long-term life journey. The pastor should listen for the way the parishioner both reveals and conceals himself in telling his story. It is important that the parishioner be able to share himself openly and be able to decide how much to share with the pastor now. Many pastors have had the experience of a person in crisis apparently sharing too much of himself and in the next visit appearing cold and resistant to relationship. The important thing is the pastoral carer's awareness not only of what is said to her, but of how the relationship with the parishioner is developing.

The listening involved in pastoral guidance also requires a sensitivity to cultural and contextual differences that may exist between the pastor and her parishioner. There may be differences in gender and assumptions about gender roles to be acknowledged. There may be racial and ethnic or other cultural differences to be understood before any guidance for the future should be offered. The pastor needs to be aware and constantly checking her assumptions about situations like the present one. What are her assumptions about illness and grief that may be different here?

What are her assumptions about what men do and what women do that may be different and thus color the way that guidance about future action may be understood? That awareness of contextual limits and biases should not paralyze her, but simply make her more realistic about her understanding of the parishioner's journey thus far and thoughts about the future.

The pastor who has been present with the parishioner, who has been sensitive and responsive to her anxiety, who has been able to listen dialogically and understand something about the parishioner's present situation and past journey is one who may offer guidance about what lies ahead. Poor guidance is usually the result of not noticing and not listening or of the pastor's own need to get satisfaction and resolve his anxiety by solving a problem. The right path for this parishioner may not be the same path that has been right for others. Pastoral guidance comes from being in the path with the one being offered guidance.

Return to the pastoral event described in chapter 1. One could question whether or not the pastor spent as much time as needed being present with the parishioner's feelings about her present situation and the story about her past life. Nevertheless, he apparently had been sufficiently present with her and her sometime irrational expectations of her daughter that she could begin to hear the pastor when he guided her to consider moving to an assisted living facility.

> **P9:** When you are up to it do you think that you at least would go see what one looks like? Just to visit and see what they do and how other older adults like you are living in those communities? I could talk with your daughter about it and also arrange it if you would like me to.

> **M9:** I guess it would not hurt to go see this place, but you need to talk to my daughter and see what she thinks. I am just so tired of trying to take care of myself and my daughter is not cooperating with me. I really need the help, this last incident was a close call and I don't think that if I were alone I would have survived. I worry about that. Talk to her and see what she says.

> **P10:** But you are willing to go visit an assisted living community?

> **M10:** If it's all right with my daughter, yes.

After hearing and responding to the particular circumstances of a person's lostness, a pastor may have established sufficient credibility and trust with his parishioner that he can effectively share some of his general knowledge that may guide her to a right path for the future.

A final point must be made about pastoral guidance, again using the image of the shepherd and the lost sheep. The goal of the shepherd is to do what is necessary to return the sheep to the flock. The goal of the pastor is to return the person—who may be separated from the faith community by grief, illness, or other circumstance—actually or symbolically to that community. She does this by representing the community through her person, by offering community through her relationship to the separated one, and, finally, by doing whatever is needed to reconnect that person to the community of faith. Thus she leads by still waters and in right paths.

Summary and Reflection

In these first three chapters pastoral care has been described as the hearing and remembering that takes place in pastoral relationships based on the conviction that God hears and remembers us. This understanding of pastoral care places a great deal of emphasis on the carer's ability to listen and understand the situation of the person cared for. It requires wisdom that was defined as a quality or capacity in caring that involves the pastor's knowing, being, and doing. The carer listens "care-fully" in order to be present with the other and to guide, or as the Twenty-third Psalm images it, to restore the soul. The carer listens in order to be present and to understand the situation of the person cared for, so that what is offered as guidance will be specific to that person, not something that might be said or suggested to anyone.

Theologically, a pastoral carer is not called to care for persons by solving their problems. He or she is called to represent, recognize, and communicate what a person really is. Care is pastoral when it looks deeper than the present situation and reminds the person cared for that he or she is a child of God created in and for relationship. What is essential for pastoral care is developing the theological and practical wisdom to do this.

The pastoral wisdom that expresses knowledge, presence, and guidance requires attention to the immediate situation of the patient or parishioner, her loss, her illness or whatever has separated her from the larger faith community. In addition to concern for the immediate problem, however, it also involves listening for the larger story of the person's life—who that person is apart from her illness, pain, or grief. The person cared for is more than what has separated her from the faith community. It is important that the pastor use his wisdom to assist the parishioner in talking about her life as well as her problem.

Following an insight offered by the Wisdom literature of the Bible, pastoral wisdom requires the carer to listen carefully to the nonreligious language of the person cared for. The Wisdom literature assumes God's presence in human life without talking much about God. Although pastoral care may involve prayer, the reading of Scripture, and verbal reminders that God does remember God's children, like much of the Wisdom literature, pastoral care most often deals with human situations expressed in ways that are not specifically religious. The carer's knowledge, presence, and guidance can most often best be demonstrated by his willingness to hear and remember the particular way a person expresses herself without trying to change that expression into religious language.

Another important clue for pastoral wisdom is the importance of listening for both the testimony and the countertestimony to faith. This insight comes from the literature of Wisdom, the Psalms, and many other places in the Bible. In Scripture and in human life there is a positive affirmation of life and faith and the negative uncertainty and doubt about God and what human life is all about. Although most of us would rather not recognize it, the word from Ecclesiastes that "vanity of vanity, all is vanity," is not an isolated message in the Bible. Neither is it isolated or unusual in the feelings of those the pastor cares for. And because the countertestimony message is uncomfortable to hear, pastoral carers are called to hear and listen more carefully to those uncomfortable words. Those without pastoral calling are much less likely to allow themselves to be sufficiently present to hear. The pastoral carer may indeed be one of the few who is willing to be present in "the darkest valley" with the patient or parishioner.

CHAPTER 4

Limit, Loss, and Grief

Blessed are they that mourn: for they shall be comforted.
—Matthew 5:4 KJV

All that has been said in the first three chapters about the presence and guidance necessary for pastoral wisdom applies to the human problems addressed in this chapter and those that follow it. The emphasis in these later chapters, however, is more on the knowledge that the carer needs to have in order to address the problems that call for pastoral ministry. There are many more human problems than can be discussed here, but those that have seemed most challenging to most pastors and their parishioners are the "dark valleys" of loss and grief, of illness, of abuse and addiction, and of family relationships. It is essential that those who care have knowledge of these human problems and develop ways of addressing them. The first of these is the challenge of limit, loss, and grief.

The darkest valley that most of us face is the valley of limit, loss, and grief; and it is often the most challenging problem that pastoral carers encounter in their ministry. How will those who mourn be comforted? Many of them will be comforted by carers whose pastoral wisdom is reflected in what they know, in what they are, and in what they do. In this chapter more will be said about what we need to know about grief and mourning than about being and doing, but all that has been said earlier about wisdom, presence, and guidance is involved in the practical knowledge of care for those facing or living with loss.

What Carers Need to Know

Learning how to respond to grief and mourning should be foremost in pastoral care, but it is important to broaden our view of grief to include many kinds of losses and the reality of human limits. We lose not only through death, but also by leaving and being left, changing, letting go, and moving on. These losses begin very early in life and many of them are necessary for our development as persons. Some of the losses that Judith Voirst points to in her practical and useful book *Necessary Losses* are very basic and simple, but it is helpful to remember them and recognize their importance.[1] Those losses include those that begin in early childhood: the facts that our mother is going to leave us, and we will leave her; that what hurts us cannot always be kissed and made better; that we will have to accept, in other people and ourselves, the mingling of love with hate, of the good with the bad; and that we are powerless to protect those we love from danger and pain, from the inroads of time, from the coming of age, and from death. These losses are a part of life. They are unavoidable and necessary because we grow by losing, leaving, and letting go. The pastoral carer's awareness of life as an ongoing process of loving and losing can deepen her pastoral relationship with the one experiencing limit and loss.

The great twentieth-century theologian Karl Barth is helpful in reminding us of the God-givenness of human limits. He speaks of humankind's limited time of life as "a unique opportunity" which must be grasped and used productively. "To be man," he said, "is to live in time. Humanity is in time."[2] But the time God gives is limited and finally comes to an end. "For at a certain point life began. Now we are somewhere in the middle or before or after the middle. One day it will be over. This is how we are in time. This is our allotted time, and no other."[3] The fact of this limit is seldom in the foreground of our experience, but it is increasingly in the background as persons move toward the end of their allotted time. Those who offer pastoral care to those who have experienced loss will be confronted with their own limit in time and the fact that they too will face the death of those whom they love and their own death. Recognition of this common humanity and the limits that all human beings share is part of the pastor's spiritual preparation for offering his or her presence in relationship.

Sigmund Freud can contribute to our understanding of limit and loss in his classic paper "Mourning and Melancholia."[4] The phenomenon of human separation from one another is universal. Ideally we address the loss of important persons by our identifying with them. Thus the pain of separation is diminished by internalizing a part of the lost person. This is similar to the way the child copes with the many small separations of parental unavailability by creating an internal representation of the parent's presence. The significance of separation for each person originates in the caregiving relationships of early life that create the psychological foundation for later relational experience. We love and we lose. Dealing with separation and loss is a lifelong phenomenon that is profoundly important because of the fundamental nature of human relationality. The value of this kind of theory is that it places limit, loss, and grief at the very beginning of the developmental process, as an integral part of it. Loss, therefore, cannot be viewed as simply an experience contradicting life—somehow an exception to the life process. It is a part of living from the beginning.

Psychiatrist and writer Robert J. Lifton underscored this theme in commenting that there is no love without loss, no moving beyond loss without some experiencing of mourning. To be unable to mourn is to be unable to enter the human cycle of death and rebirth. The capacity to deal with separation facilitates growth by permitting an openness to losing the familiar, be it people or their support.[5] The pastor who can effectively comfort must be aware of the fact of limit and loss in human life and also be aware of his own losses. He must know about the way that persons grieve and mourn.

Although grief and mourning are similar in meaning, it can be useful to distinguish them. The term "grieving" can best be used to refer to all of the possible ways that persons respond to the losses that occur in their lives. Mourning is a somewhat narrower term that refers to what persons do individually and socially to cope with loss and to transform the relationship to what or who has been lost. It is very important that pastoral wisdom include some general knowledge of grief and the mourning process that is informed by those who have done research and written about it.

One of the most influential interpretations of the grief process has been Erich Lindemann's pioneering study, "Symptomatology and Management of Acute Grief," published in *The American Journal of Psychiatry* in September 1944. In that article Lindemann affirmed grief as "work," something necessary for life rather than something pathological that should be avoided. He described five things that he had observed in acute grief: (1) bodily distress; (2) preoccupation with the image of the deceased; (3) guilt; (4) anger; and (5) loss of customary patterns of conduct. On the basis of these observations, he theorized that there are discernible stages in the grief process that the grieving person and those who care for that person should be aware of.

Hospital chaplain Granger Westberg's little book *Good Grief*, which was published in 1962, is one of the books that established Lindemann's stages of grief as a part of popular pastoral wisdom. Westberg presented them as the titles of his book's chapters: We are in a state of shock. We express emotion. We feel depressed and very lonely. We may experience physical symptoms of distress. We may become panicky. We feel a sense of guilt about the loss. We are filled with hostility and resentment. We are unable to return to usual activities. Gradually hope comes through. We struggle to readjust to reality.[6]

The Lindemann study of grief work concerned those who had lost someone close to them through death. Elisabeth Kübler-Ross's research, some twenty-five years later, studied the grief of terminally ill persons grieving their own dying. Both perspectives are important for the pastor who ministers to the grieving and the dying. According to Kübler-Ross the dying patient goes through the following stages in mourning his own death: denial, anger, bargaining, depression, and acceptance.[7] These stages, somewhat fewer than Lindemann's, have become even more familiar in popular and in pastoral literature. Unfortunately, they have sometimes been accepted as the way a person is supposed to die. Certainly, some general knowledge of things to expect in the mourning process is helpful, but these stages are not universal and do not always occur in the sequence that Kübler-Ross has suggested.

Using stages as a means of understanding the grief process, however, tends to take away some of the individuality of the experience of loss—the way that it happens somewhat differently for each person or culture as well as some of the important communal dimensions of the mourning process. Larry R. Churchill has argued that to put dying into stages is placing theory over personal meaning and denying the dying person the opportunity to tell what dying means to him. Only the dying person himself can say what death means to him and how he wishes to cope with it. Putting the dying person into a stage may help reduce the carer's anxiety, but it distances the carer from the one he is attempting to care for and makes a genuine relationship more difficult.

Rather than stages, Churchill emphasizes story as a category of interpretation for the experience of dying that is logically prior to "stage." Although he acknowledges that the dying do the things that Kübler-Ross's stages describe, he insists that more important than knowing that a dying person is in the bargaining stage is for him to be able to share with a caring person "what they are bargaining for, with what, and with whom." The fact that he is in a stage gives only a shell of an answer as to where the dying person is. It excludes the personal and idiosyncratic and in doing so is disrespectful of the dying person. Churchill concludes:

> The notion of the dying as teachers and helpers reaffirms a communal framework for human meaning. . . . The emphasis on community is essential because it acknowledges our interdependence with the dying. The dying need to be part of a community, to be sure, but it is also true that the dying can teach and support the communities of which they are a part. [8]

Some more recent studies have focused on grief that is "unrecognized and unsanctioned" or "disenfranchised" because it takes place in unauthorized grief and grievers.[9] For example, grief for family members has been strongly legitimated in the literature, but the importance of grieving over the loss of close friends is seldom recognized as often having similar intensity. The need for grief work has also often been overlooked according to authors like Vanderlyn R. Pine and Kenneth J. Doka in children, homosexual and heterosexual persons living in out-of-wedlock intimacy, rape victims, and adult survivors of child sexual abuse, particularly those who have kept the assault secret, AIDS victims who have hidden the nature of their illness, prenatal death, and birth mothers who have given up their infants. The implication for the pastoral carer is that grief and mourning may be found in unexpected persons and places and that those called to care should be on the lookout for grief and grievers wherever they are.

Most of the theories of grief and mourning that have been discussed thus far have dealt with the earlier stages of the grief process. Not all grief, however, is acute grief. There is a process of grief and mourning that needs to be attended to after the intensity of acute grieving has passed. Offering care early in the process is essential and makes possible the pastoral care that may come later. Also, some of the things that have been said about stages in the grief process are important reminders that what is helpful at one point in the process may not be at another point.

Philosopher Thomas Attig has examined and interpreted the longer process of grief as an effort at "relearning the world."[10] This is an image or theme that can be particularly useful for pastoral carers who have an ongoing pastoral responsibility for persons beyond the early days after the death or loss. Like Churchill, Attig emphasizes particular stories of loss rather than stages, and this emphasis is much in keeping with the character of the pastoral relationship. "No story of loss," he reminds us, "replicates any other." What is important is to

> learn the details of the story each survivor has to tell about how the loss has changed profoundly his or her experience of the world and has limited what is possible in the next chapters of each biography. You must learn the different ways the death disrupts the flow of each survivor's life story. You must learn how each survivor faces distinct challenges and struggles to go on in the next chapters of life.[11]

This is the kind of knowledge that is important for pastoral wisdom in dealing with limit, loss, and grief. Through hearing and responding to the stories, caregivers can assist the grieving person to identify the variety of psychological, behavioral, physical, social, intellectual, and spiritual challenges that he or she faces in relearning the world. The mourner relearns how to live in the physical world without the deceased and how to act in a social world that no longer includes the one who has been lost. Relearning the world involves relearning one's self without the other and learning new ways to remember and experience the one who has died. Caregivers can motivate and encourage the mourner to engage actively in coping at his or her own pace and in ways that fit with who he or she has been and hopes to be. The carer can help identify options and effective means of addressing the particular challenges in the mourner's unique life circumstance.

Attig offers a critique of stage theory that is somewhat different from Churchill's. He says that because the stages appear static this may suggest to the grieving person that the course of his life is in some way predetermined and thus reinforce a sense of passivity and helplessness.[12] Grieving is an active, not a static, process. Helping actions are those that respect individuality and address this helplessness.[13] Effective grieving makes it possible for mourners to remember their loss without intense pain and anguish and to cherish memories of those they have cared about. It is possible, Attig says, for survivors to enjoy a transformed, dynamic, and sustaining relationship with those who have died through continued interaction with the story of their lives.

Relearning the world in the grieving process is learning how to be and act in the world differently in the light of loss. Human beings develop their individual character through their patterns of caring and through the variety, breadth, and depth of their attachments to the surrounding world. Their life histories unfold as they weave and reweave these threads of attachment. Bereavement rends, and sometimes threatens to completely unravel, the fabric of caring involvement in the world. In the grieving process, the mourner struggles to reweave the fabric of life and establish a new integrity in his pattern of caring involvement.[14]

The effective mourner becomes different in the light of the loss as she learns to assume a new orientation to the world. Effective grieving understood as a relearning process is far from a simply cognitive affair. It is the whole person that is involved and thus it is learning how to be and act as well as to think. The grieving person relearns by looking for new ways to establish coherence in present living, to complete her life story, and to find ways of seeing herself as part of a community larger than herself.

An important part of Attig's description of grief as a process of relearning is his discussion of the survivor's relearning his relationships to the deceased. We lose the presence of the central character or characters in the ongoing stories of our lives. We lose the usual ways of connecting with those who have died, but we learn to continue to love the person of the one who has died, experienced not as something fixed in time or memory but as one who retains the power to move us even as we survive him or her. We continue to love and cherish the stories of a life or lives that have now been completed.[15] He quotes from C. S. Lewis's *A Grief Observed:*

> Bereavement is a universal and integral part of our experience of love. It follows marriage as normally as marriage follows courtship or as autumn follows summer. It is not a truncation of the process but one of its phases; not interruption of the dance, but the next figure.[16]

What Carers Need to Be

All of this knowledge and more is essential for caregivers in responding to acute grief and to the long-term process of mourning, but knowledge is only one part of pastoral wisdom. A number of years ago in a summer course in pastoral care, one of the students was not doing well in the parts of the course that required accurate writing and the understanding of written materials. There was one exam question, however, that did not require much theoretical knowledge. It simply asked the student to describe how he would respond to a particular situation of acute grief. On that question this C-minus student on theory made an A with his very simple, but fully present answer. "It is not my policy," he wrote,

> to ask someone, lest (sic) pray when they have lost their loved one. For this very same person may have prayed more than I have ever prayed. In this case, I would rather be Silence. For I remember when my father die, many people come and say, "you have my deepest sympathy," but one person come to me without any words of sympathy or quotation of scripture to me. He sat with me. When I would stand up, he stood up. If I walk to the door, he would also walk to the door. I have never been so comforted and warmed by Christian love as I was at that moment. It reminded me of Jesus when Mary came to him weeping and said, Lord if you had been here my brother would not died. Jesus did not say a word, but groaned in the spirit. Not many people at this time want someone

56

to pray for them but your Present and Silence is the best expression for pray at that time.[17]

This response to acute grief, more than anything else, emphasizes the importance of presence and all that has been said about it earlier in this book.

The importance of presence, of simply being there and representing God and the faith community can also be underscored by reference to the human expressions of loss, grief, and protest in the Bible. The book of Lamentations and many of the psalms are laments that pastors should acknowledge and attend to in their spiritual preparation for ministry to those who mourn. As described by Old Testament scholar Kathleen O'Connor, the laments of the Bible are prayers that erupt from wounds, burst out of unbearable pain, and bring that pain to language. They complain, shout, protest, and take anger and despair before God and the community. "Although laments appear disruptive of God's world," O'Connor says, "they are acts of fidelity. In vulnerability and honesty, they cling obstinately to God and demand for God to see, hear, and act."[18] In Lamentations God does not respond to the laments that are expressed.

> Lamentations refuses denial, practices truth-telling, and reverses amnesia. It invites reader into pain, chaos, and brutality, both human and divine. It conveys the effect of trauma, loss, and grief beyond tears. Because God's voice is absent, it gives primacy to suffering voices like no other biblical book.[19]

In their presence with those who grieve and lament, those who care need to be aware that in the book of Lamentations and in many of the psalms there is no responsive voice of comfort offering relief. Similarly, in much of the carer's presence in the midst of acute grief, there needs to be silence. Most important is that the anguish be heard without a comforting correction that in effect denies or reduces the pain. That is a hard lesson to learn because the calling of caregivers is to comfort and restore the soul, but the message of this part of the Bible and of psychological studies of grief as well is that attempts at comfort before the pain and despair have been heard are no comfort at all. The task of the carer is to be present in the Twenty-third Psalm's darkest valley.

Although it is important that the carer learn to be silent in the midst of acute grief, it is also important that his or her spiritual preparation for ministry to the grief sufferer include some ongoing dialogue with the Christian message about death and eternal life. This requires some serious reading and study, preferably in dialogue with other members of one's faith community. The resources for study will vary from carer to carer. What is important is that the study is an ongoing process of preparation for ministry. The following are two examples of modern Christian theologians who have contributed to our understanding of loss and death.

Daniel Migliore reminds us that human relationality makes us particularly vulnerable to the losses involved in death; that Christian confidence in the face of death is based not on human accomplishments or belief in immortality, but the grace of God as revealed in Jesus Christ, from which nothing can separate us. It is important for us to be aware of the present incompleteness of the work of redemption and that God's final victory over evil is to come in the future.[20]

Writing about eschatology and pastoral care, Jürgen Moltmann has said:

> The soul is not immortal but the *spirit of God* is immortal, which already here, in this life, fills believers with the power of the Resurrection (Rom. 8:11). Wherever the life-giving Spirit is experienced, there eternal life is experienced before death. Wherever persons get close to the creative ground of lived life, death disappears and they experience continuance without perishing. . . . Death . . . is neither the separation of the soul from the body nor the end of body and soul but the transformation of the spirit of life, which fills body and soul, into the new, transfigured world-order of God.[21]

These theological affirmations are intended to challenge the pastoral carer to engage in a continual search for theological resources to address the dark valley of loss and grief. The theologians' words are not necessarily words to be spoken to the grieving, but they can contribute to the wisdom that the carer offers through his or her presence. What seems most important in the theology touched on here is that death is not a final separation from relationship and care. Different resources may be more helpful to other Christian carers. If one is committed to care, then one must be familiar with the message that informs that care and that the carer represents. One can offer pastoral care effectively without knowing the message well, but the dialogue with the message of faith must be alive and well.

What Carers Need to Do

In the early or acute parts of the grieving process, carers need to be present and mostly silent. At later points in the process guidance can be expressed in ways that involve words and actions as well as presence. Carers who can be present and silent in the midst of acute grief are much more likely to offer comforting and insightful words when words become appropriate. As has been suggested earlier, the most important element in guidance is "care-full" listening to determine where the person or parishioner is in his journey through the grieving process.

In offering guidance to a person involved in the process of mourning it is important to remember what was said earlier, namely, that guiding is not directing the person's life but *reminding* the person cared for of specific resources that have been part of his life, though they are now absent or weak. Guiding is aimed less at acquiring new information than recovering old resources. In all that the pastor does in offering guidance, she is attempting to help the grieving person overcome his sense of helplessness or what psychiatrist Jerome Frank has called "demoralization."[22] It is the feeling of being unable to cope, to feel powerless to change the situation or themselves. According to dictionaries demoralized persons are deprived of spirit, disheartened, confused, and bewildered. Theologically, this condition calling for guidance is, in the terms of the Twenty-third Psalm, "restoring the soul," the life and breath of the person.

The pastor does this by recognizing that effective grieving is active. She attempts to support the parishioner's action by discussing specific tasks—the things that seem possible and those that might be possible in the future. These may be things that the person has never done for himself before, things as simple as cleaning house, preparing meals, and the like. It may involve reminding him of unused skills that have been available to him in the past or noticing and supporting specific tasks that have been accomplished in the present. These kinds of specific responses avoid the empty reassurance that "everything will be all right" and require that the pastor has listened and remembered the larger story of the grieving person's life.

The pastor also supports action by encouraging the person to make choices rather than the pastor choosing or deciding for them. Choosing to do almost anything is an action, and action helps to defeat helplessness and demoralization. The carer also supports the action of reentry into old and new relationships. She doesn't push this, but she listens, talks about it, and looks for ways to make this action easier through friends and resources of the church. She uses her knowledge of the parishioner's life to discuss recovering old purposes and finding new ones.

The pastor guides by helping the mourner explore the story of the life that has ended. Because that person is no longer present to tell his or her story it is important to find other ways to do this, such as soliciting letters and stories about him or her from friends and associates. The pastor has in all probability done this in preparing for the funeral, but this remembering of the life of the deceased is important for the mourner long after this. The pastoral carer is, in effect, helping the mourner not forget, but develop a new relationship to the one who has been lost. In relationship, the pastor and the mourner reflect on the abiding meaning of the life that has ended and on God's promises not to be separated from that life. All that is involved in this kind of guidance is dependent on the "care-full" listening that enables the pastor to learn and celebrate the story.

Summary and Reflection

The goal of the pastor in guidance is always relational. His concern is to restore the person, who may be separated from the faith community by her loss and grief, actually or symbolically, to that community. He does this by representing the community through his person, by offering community through his relationship to the separated one, and, finally, by doing whatever is needed to reconnect that person to the community of faith. Using the image of the shepherd and the lost sheep, the goal of the shepherd is to do what is necessary to return the sheep to the flock.

CHAPTER 5

Care for the Sick

The human spirit will endure sickness; but a broken spirit—who can bear?
—Proverbs 18:14

A re any among you sick? They should call for the elders of the church and have them pray over them, anointing them with oil in the name of the Lord" (James 5:14). James is a book that focuses on what the Christian should do. Pastoral wisdom, however, involves not only doing, but being and knowing as well. This chapter touches on all three, but emphasizes what the carer needs to be and to know in order to act in ways most likely to restore the soul of the sick. Again, the kind of knowledge of illness that is discussed is not academic knowledge valuable for its own sake, but knowledge to be employed in being and doing.

A hospital chaplain once commented that the warmest appreciation for his ministry that came to him from patients and families was, "You never seemed in a hurry." This certainly does not mean that visits to the sick must be long visits, but it does mean that one of the most important things that a pastor brings to those who are separated from their customary life by illness is his or her patience. The pastor whose visits convey primarily how busy he or she is with other things is not able to do much toward restoring the soul of the one who is ill.

What Carers for the Sick Need to Know—
About Themselves

The terms "patience" and "patient" are both derived from the Latin word that means to suffer or to endure and from which the term "compassion" is also derived.[1] "Compassion" has been described as "the virtue by which we have a sympathetic consciousness of sharing the distress or suffering of another person." Compassion has within it a large portion of self-awareness—awareness of one's own feelings as well as the feelings of another. Such awareness may best be described as the carer's knowledge of his own "patienthood," that is, in spite of the illness that separates them, he is not so different from the patient after all. The words of psychiatrist Harry Stack Sullivan, known for his treatment of those with the most severe mental illness, can be a helpful reminder to all who care for those with illness of any kind; he said "We are all more human than otherwise."

The carer's awareness of her own patienthood is a major contributor to developing patience, one of the most important elements in ministry to the sick. It is not, however, an invitation for the carer to talk about her own illnesses to the person to whom she offers care. Rather it is an invitation for the pastor to be aware of her own vulnerability and her own need for care. Carers can be more patient when they are aware of themselves as patients. Although their limitation or vulnerability to illness may not be evident or in the foreground of the carer's experience, their awareness of it and their ability to allow it to be seen is an important part of their ability to care. This mingling together what it means to be a patient who is ill and the experience of learning to be patient is valuable practical knowledge in the pastoral care of the sick. It is her patience that allows the carer to hear and remember, which is the essence of pastoral care.

What Carers Need to Know—About the Patient

In addition to the carer's knowledge of herself as a patient—knowledge that helps generate compassion and patience, the pastoral carer needs to have some knowledge of what the patient himself may be feeling. One of the most striking descriptions of the experience of illness comes from the writer Susan Sontag who speaks of illness as "the night-side of life," an "onerous citizenship."

> Everyone who is born holds dual citizenship, in the kingdom of the well and in the kingdom of the sick. Although we all prefer to use only the good passport, sooner or later each of us is obliged, at least for a spell, to identify ourselves as citizens of that other place.[2]

The place Sontag speaks of symbolically is the place of illness itself, wherever the patient may be physically. There are, however, some special things that are experienced when the place of illness is an institution like a hospital. The hospital as well as the illness has a special impact on the patient. The fact of being admitted to a hospital usually reflects a crisis in the life of the patient and his or her family. Growing out of his own experience as a hospital patient, Liston Mills wrote:

> The crisis has at least two dimensions: the fact of the illness with its attendant uncertainties, pains, disruptions, and distress, and the crisis of the hospital, a strange environment to most patients, reflecting an unaccustomed social world inhabited by apparently efficient people, speaking a strange language, and determining among themselves how the patient's life is to be ordered. [3]

The patient has been designated as "sick," a "patient," a "case," and thus suddenly or gradually loses the illusion of health, adequacy, and control of her life. There is a loss of status and a kind of depersonalization. Whereas society values competence and independence, illness confirms the patient as weak, helpless, and in need of care. A person whose life was formerly characterized by self-sufficiency can be quickly transformed into one defined by symptoms of the illness, discomfort, and incapacity. This betrayal of the self by the body diminishes self-esteem and dislocates the patient from life as she has known it.

Removal from family and friends can itself provoke a crisis of self-understanding. The patient's network of support is replaced by a community of strangers who are specially uniformed for their function and who may seem to see the patient as a particular kind of case rather than as a person. This professional presence may provide some security, but it does not offer the personal support usually given by family and friends. These circumstances of hospitalization contribute to the patient's anxiety and his apprehension both about the treatment of his illness and the implications of this for his life in the future.

This anxiety is sometimes intensified by the sense that doctors and families are withholding information and making decisions behind the patient's back. When this is the case, the uncertainty involved makes coming to terms with the illness and a general sense of hopefulness about life more difficult. It is frequently compounded by questions about finances and insurance and questions about the course of one's life after hospitalization.

What Carers Can Do

What the pastoral carer can offer in helping the patient address the crisis of hospitalization is not limited to the prayer and anointing recommendation of the book of James. A newspaper reporter observing a particular pastor's ministry in a hospital setting described the pastor as "supportive, helpful, and not in the way, all at the same time." These words may provide a useful guide for what good hospital visitation should be.

Although "not being in the way" may simply seem to be a negative injunction, it underscores the fact that the hospital visitor comes to the hospital as an outsider. That fact needs to be recognized in a number of practical ways. Pastoral visits, for example, should ordinarily not be very long; fifteen or twenty minutes is often sufficient, and more can easily become a burden to the patient, especially when he or she is tired or in some discomfort. Though hospital visits may on occasion develop into extended pastoral conversation about life issues, they are best viewed primarily not as counseling occasions requiring extended time, but as simple, symbolically rich opportunities for being present with the patient and family in a concerned and supportive way.

Because the hospital visitor is an outsider, it is also appropriate and important that the visitor, lay or ordained, identify himself or herself to persons in authority on the floor where the patient is located, indicating that he or she is a pastor or lay visitor who has come to see a particular patient. Persons who will be visiting regularly in a particular hospital unit should usually become acquainted with the person in charge of that unit or the nurse regularly assigned to the care of the patient being visited. Such a procedure is respectful of the authority of the nursing staff and allows them to advise the visitor of any limitations on visitation or procedures that need to be observed. It also respects the authority of the visitor as one having an appropriate reason to be with the patient, and the hospital staff can prevent or reduce unnecessary interruptions to the visit. It is important that hospital visitors be allies in the care of the patient and family and not in the way.

All of the skills that the visitor may have developed as a listener can be useful in hospital conversation. Perhaps most important is being responsive to the patient's present feelings and state of mind rather than trying to make him or her be some other way. If patients or families are sad, they probably have good reason for being so, and the visitor can be most helpful by responding sensitively to that mood rather than trying to change it. If the patient or family is cheered by the visit, it is most likely that this occurs because of the visitor being with them where they are rather than bringing in cheer from the outside. The helpfulness of the visitor may also include doing things for the patient or family that they are not prepared to do for themselves. The major caution about this is that the visitor follow the lead of the patient rather than deciding beforehand what needs to be done.

Once the initial shock of illness and hospitalization passes, patients may begin to develop coping strategies to deal with the fact of their illness. Assimilation of the fact of pain and diminished self-esteem fosters despair or the discovery of ways to deal with a new situation. The carer can be of considerable assistance in this quest. For example, anything a patient can do to assume responsibility for his or her treatment enhances their self-respect and decreases his or her sense of isolation and loneliness. Encouragement to request information concerning the procedures being utilized serves to enable the patient to participate in his or her treatment. The opportunity to assess one's illness and to consider possible outcomes also increases one's sense of control. Such occasions also grant patients permission to grieve the possible loss of function or potential as they become aware of the realities of their condition. Such attentiveness may also provide a setting for patients to begin to reflect on the meaning of their illness and to anticipate a future.

In addition to being helpful and not in the way, hospital visitation should be supportive. This means that the visitation is primarily intended to maintain continuity of relationship and prior religious meanings rather than to confront the patient with new things to be done in life or faith. There may be some exceptions to this view, but insisting on change in the patient through aggressive religious witness or other means is generally inappropriate in a hospital setting. A supportive visit is one that enables the patient or family to maintain the faith in, and relational connections to, those things that are most important to them. The lay or ordained hospital visitor is a representative of religious meanings and community and offers support to the patient primarily through serving as a reminder of them.

It is in this context that the question of prayer with patients is best understood. Although the anointing spoken of in the book of James is not a customary practice in most Christian traditions, prayer by the pastoral visitor in the hospital is a strong ritual expectation of many church members who may feel hurt or deprived if the pastor or the lay minister does not offer to pray with and for them. On the other hand, prayer is not always wanted or appreciated and sometimes meets strong objection. A simple question will usually suffice to determine what is most appropriate and helpful. In situations where prayer is explicitly requested, it is often helpful to talk briefly about the request itself and what the person is seeking through it. In any case, when prayer is offered, it is important that it express something of the life situation as experienced by the patient and family, including their hopes, fears, and desires (without resorting to magical or unrealistic thought), while also setting these human concerns in the context of the mystery of God's reality and love. This is often especially meaningful if done, in part, in the language of the psalms and other Scripture. The prayer thus helps to remind patient and family of what they already know in faith, and supports them with the specific resources of the tradition in their hour of special need.[4]

More Things for the Carer to Know

Being a patient means dealing with pain, and being a pastor requires knowledge about pain even though that knowledge is nearly impossible to obtain secondhand. Elaine Scarry has described physical pain as "unlike any other state of consciousness" in that it has no content that can be referred to. It is not of or for anything. More than any other phenomenon it resists objectification in language. She is very helpful in reminding the carer about the difficulties of understanding and responding to another person's pain.

> One might almost appear to be speaking about two wholly distinct orders of events. For the person whose pain it is, it is "effortlessly" grasped (that is, even with the most heroic effort it cannot *not* be grasped); while for the person outside the sufferer's body, what is "effortless" is *not* grasping it (it is easy to remain wholly unaware of its existence; even with effort). . . . For the person in pain . . . "having pain" may come to be thought of as the most vibrant example of what it is to "have certainty," while for the other person it is so elusive that "hearing about pain" may exist as the primary model of what it is "to have doubt."[5]

These striking words should be humbling to the carer, reminding her that she can have little understanding of what the patient is experiencing, but nevertheless is called to "be there." They also remind us not only of the isolation that pain may bring, but of the particularities of a person's experience of illness. Knowing some things about what it means to be a patient is valuable, but pastors should recognize the particularities of each illness as well as the common experience of illness. Moreover, illness has different meanings in different cultures.

Psychiatrist and ethnographer Arthur Kleinman has noted that the cultural meanings that mark the sick person often stamp him with a meaning of his illness that may be unwanted and neither easily warded off nor coped with. "People vary in the resources available to them to resist or rework the cultural meanings of illness. Those meanings present a problem to patient, family, and practitioner every bit as difficult as the lesion itself."[6] Attempting to take cultural, contextual variations into account in responding to patients can be one of the pastoral carer's important tasks.

67

In listening to patients, Eric J. Cassell has identified three kinds of things that the carer needs to know: (1) the natural facts of a person's life; (2) his or her values or the contextual factors necessary to interpret those facts; and (3) what Cassell has called aesthetic knowledge or the kind of life that a person has created. Cassell thinks of life as a work of art and a person's choices in life as a means of creation. The life created by those choices may be ugly or beautiful, profoundly moving or uninspiring, but it is important for the patient and for the helping person to look for and find a way of speaking about the aesthetic pattern that has been created by that life.[7] Most of the patients that a pastor visits will not need to know what Cassell means by aesthetic knowledge, but they will have some sense of the life that they have created and will often have the need to share some of their creation.

An example of this comes from a student in clinical pastoral education, a Japanese woman who was intuitively skilled at listening to patients and helping them tell their stories. As a student chaplain in a large general hospital, she was visiting an old Georgia farmer nearing eighty who, among other things, told her that when he was growing up his family was so poor that they couldn't have biscuits for breakfast; they had to eat corn bread. In spite of the fact that she had grown up with rice instead of either biscuits or corn bread, this pastoral carer was able to sense the "aesthetic knowledge"—something about the life this man had created—that was revealed in this brief story. Approaching death, the elderly patient was celebrating with this young woman how far he had been able to come in his life. He had grown up with corn bread. Now his life was full of biscuits made with white flour.

Another variable in the meaning of illness that the carer should be aware of is the patient's need to tell the story of his illness. Arthur Frank, writing out of the experience of his own illness, speaks powerfully both to those who are ill and those attempting to care for them. He speaks to the patient about the loss the illness often brings:

> Let yourself grieve your losses and . . . find people who will accept that grieving. . . . The losses you go through are real, and no one should take these away from you. They are a part of your experience, and you are entitled to them. Illness can teach that every part of life is worth experiencing, even the losses. To grieve well is to

68

value what you have lost. When you value even the feeling of loss, you value life itself, and you begin to live again.[8]

Frank is convinced that those who are not ill now need to see and hear what illness is, which ultimately means seeing and hearing what life is. In terms of what has been discussed earlier in this chapter, the carer needs to be aware of his own patienthood.

> The mutual responsibilities of the ill to express and the healthy to hear meet in the recognition that our creativity depends on our frailty. Life without illness would not just be incomplete, it would be impossible. The paradox is that illness must remain painful, even to those who fully believe its necessity.[9]

These are important words for any who attempt to minister to the sick.

Those who are sick may tell their story in different ways. Warren Thomas Reich has described these ways of telling their story as the languages of suffering. The first language that may be heard from the sufferer is often a lament—a "language" discussed earlier in the previous chapter on limit, loss, and grief. The complaining quality of the lament can be difficult for the pastoral carer to hear, but it is simply giving voice to one's suffering, and can clearly be beneficial. "The Psalms of lament, for example, are not lyrics of submissiveness but the sufferers' expression of their own innocence, of their desire to be heard, of their petition for a sustaining, caring presence. The voice of lament can play a crucial role in growth through and beyond suffering."[10]

Suffering's second and most familiar language is story. The story grows out of relationship with a caring person and must be recounted in dialogue. Telling the story of one's suffering is a means of reforming the mute experience of suffering and carrying out the important task that was described by Arthur Frank. What is important for the carer to remember is that the suffering person tells his story in the hope that he will be able to reconstruct and thus recreate his painful and dislocating past, gain some distance from it or put it into perspective, and thus "possess" the experience as a way of putting the past behind him.

The story may also be told in order that the caring person may affirm the sufferer in the search for a new story, a story that will account for and justify a new self that might emerge from the suffering (pain, trauma, and so on) with wholeness, pride, meaning, or at least with hope. The third language of suffering is interpretive language. It is spoken in order to interpret and understand the suffering. The sufferer is a victim or a victor, a fighter or a survivor, somewhat like wrestling Jacob who, having prevailed in his struggle, is given a new name.[11]

Some Stories of Sickness

Some of the things that have been discussed in this chapter can be considered more practically by looking at situations of illness presented for discussion by pastoral carers in a clinical pastoral education program. The response made by the chaplain or carer to the patient is left blank so that the reader can imagine what she might say to this patient if she were the chaplain or her pastor. It is true that not being able to see what each person says makes the conversation more difficult to follow. On the other hand, in contrast to a verbatim dialogue where one can simply be critical of what someone else has done, this has the advantage of challenging one to concentrate on each comment that the patient makes and consider what an appropriate pastoral response might be. It is important to remember that there is no one correct response and that any response would vary according to the caregiver's relationship to the patient. Both of the events presented here have been used for teaching purposes in a seminary course on pastoral care.

In the first situation the patient is the forty-one-year-old mother of three children under the age of ten, who was diagnosed as having metastatic cancer during surgery a week before this visit. She was in the intensive care unit (ICU) for several days and then transferred to the regular nursing unit. The chaplain first visited with the patient's husband, who was distraught about his wife's condition and prognosis. He and his wife are heavily involved in the church. His comments to the pastor related to his concern for his wife, and the fact that there were many people praying for her recovery. One of the things the chaplain remembers him saying was that his wife's illness was to God's glory.

The student chaplain visited the patient after her transfer from the ICU.

Chaplain: Hello, Mrs. Simpson, I'm one of the chaplains here. I met with your husband while you were in the intensive care unit. I just wanted to stop by and see how you are doing.

Patient: I'm doing okay, I guess.

C2:

P2: They tell me that I need to stay until I can eat enough. *(There was a period of silence while the chaplain waited to see where this might lead. Patient starts to quietly cry.)* I know that this is the Lord's will, and I know that this is to his glory. *(Silence. The chaplain waited to see if the patient would continue.)* I pray for healing, but I know that he gave me this for his glory and to witness to him.

C3:

P3: *(Still crying quietly)* I just want to be well and see my children grow up, but I know God has given me this to witness for him. I just want to do God's will, and if this is necessary to show his glory, then I am happy to do this.

C4: *(After a response to P3 the chaplain asked about prayer.)*

P4: Just pray for strength and trust in God for healing.

C5:

There can be no single or simple response to offer in this situation. The pastoral carer is a minister of the Lord who leads beside still waters and restores the soul, but he does this most effectively when his patient or parishioner can say of him, "Even though I walk through the darkest valley, I fear no evil; for you are with me." The pastor's greatest temptation is to move quickly away from the darkest valley to the still waters—to hear or respond only to the religious words of faith and not the secular words of uncertainty and doubt. Responding only to the voice of testimony and not countertestimony is to suggest that we doubt that God can be with us and our parishioners in the darkest valley. Pastoral wisdom requires that we learn to be present and respond to the counter-testimony that we hear from those estranged from what is most familiar to them and not rush in too quickly to offer words of comfort.

Much more could be said about appropriate pastoral responses to this event, and it would be said in a group devoted to the ongoing learning of pastoral care. We can leave it here with the familiar questions: what does the pastor need to know, to be, and to do in responding to this very difficult situation?

The second pastoral event is one that has been particularly useful in encouraging those who discussed it to respond to the countertestimony as well as the testimony of a person's story. It is quite short in written length, but long on challenge to hear both voices. Again we have only the words of the patient. That makes it harder to follow as a pastoral conversation, but it gives the reader an opportunity to think about how he or she might understand and respond to the different themes that are present in what the patient says.

Mr. L. is a retired typesetter and graphic arts designer who is terminally ill with lung cancer. He seems pleased to have a visit from the new pastor at the church and appears to be quite ready to talk openly about his limited life expectancy and approaching death. After some introductory remarks he says:

Mr. L.: I don't want to die in the winter. I want to hold on until spring.

Pastor 1:

L2: Winter is so dreary. I don't want to be buried on a day like this. Wouldn't this be an awful day to have a funeral? (*It is cold and rainy on the day of this visit.*)

P2:

L3: Yep, I want to be buried in the spring.

P3:

L4: Yes, and I've talked to God about it and I believe he is going to grant my prayer. I really do.

P4:

L5: Well, I don't go to church like I should. I hope God has for-given me. I've asked him to. But I've always had faith. Unfortunately, I've not accessed it throughout my life as I should have.

P5:

L6: Yeah, I just wish I had done it sooner.

P6:

In this pastoral event there is testimony and countertestimony that appear in a number of different ways. There is the literal voice and the symbolic one, the practical voice that talks about the weather and the seasons and the one that reflects on the meaning of life and death. There is the testimony of the patient's faith and the countertestimony of his doubt that he has been good enough or expressed his faith soon enough. Pastoral wisdom calls on the carer to hear both kinds of voices, to see how he listens for the words of the story and for their longer-term meaning. And as always there is the potential conflict of whether the pastor should open up the possibilities here or, in the interest of time or responsibility for the whole flock, to close them off and maybe come back later.

Summary and Reflection

The book of James called on the sick to reach out and ask for the ministry of the church in their illness. This kind of initiative may or may not take place, what is essential for pastoral care in situations of illness is the carer's knowledge, presence, and guidance. The carer needs to know something about illness. She needs to find the best ways to be present in spite of the separation from community that illness creates. She needs to guide through her hearing the patient's story and remembering him as someone who is more than a patient. This kind of knowing, being, and doing can contribute significantly to the restoring of the patient's soul.

CHAPTER 6

Abuse of Self and Others

If you do abuse them, when they cry out to me, I will surely heed their cry.
—Exodus 22:23

T his chapter, like those that preceded it, addresses one of the significant problems calling for pastoral wisdom—abuse of self through addiction and abuse of others through physical, sexual, and emotional violence. What has been presented earlier about the care of the dying, the grieving, and the sick has been intended both for the ordained pastor and the lay minister of pastoral care. In this chapter and those that follow on care of the family and on pastoral counseling, the focus is more on the pastor. Certainly, much of what is discussed here has relevance for the lay carer as well, but in relation to the problem of abuse, the authority given to the ordained pastor or pastor in charge is particularly relevant for what the carer needs to be. In situations of abuse, the clergy have more authority than lay ministers to structure or define the necessary conditions for care. A pastor is better able to be tough and to say no when that is necessary. This is not a comfortable part of the pastoral role, but in situations of abuse it is often a necessary one.

Much of what is discussed here involves alcohol and other addictions, but these topics will be discussed under the heading of abuse because they most often come to the attention of the pastor when their condition has become abusive for the addicted person or others. Because the concern of this guide has been on ways of expressing care, it is a natural extension of this concern to discuss the abuse of self and others in terms of the failure to care. The situations specifically addressed here are abuse of self through substance abuse and addiction, and the physical, sexual, or emotional abuse of persons over whom the abuser has power or control. Abuse means literally "to take away from use"—to misuse or mistreat and perhaps to injure. The chapter, therefore, is concerned with the misuse and mistreatment of persons, the abused and the abuser.

Faced with a situation involving abuse of self and others, pastoral care as hearing and remembering takes on a somewhat different meaning. The pain of the present is important, but the pattern revealed by the past may be even more important. The ongoing care of the pastor may need to be expressed by remembering and confronting the abuser or the abused person with the fact that this has happened before and that the abuse is not to be minimized and denied. It must be addressed—and addressed now—with action or it will be repeated, and there may be serious or fatal consequences. What does the wise pastor need to know, to do, and to be in order to deal with the abuse of self or others?

Abuse of Self

Perhaps the most frequent problem of abuse that the pastor must deal with is the abuse of self with alcohol or other drugs. It is not unusual for the pastor to confront a situation like the following one. A leading member of the church council has been observed to be unpredictable in his attendance at important meetings and apparently unable to follow through with responsibilities he has undertaken for the church. The pastor calls the church member, Jim Jeffries, and asks if he can meet with him to discuss the difficulties that Mr. Jeffries may be having in getting the job done. When he stops by the Jeffries house the next evening, the pastor discovers that Jim has been drinking heavily and has forgotten their appointment. Mr. Jeffries apologizes profusely and asks to meet with the pastor the next afternoon. He keeps this appointment, and after a brief discussion of the responsibilities that he has undertaken and how he plans to meet them, the pastor asks him about his drinking.

Jim: I don't think it's anything to worry about, Reverend. I've just been under a lot of pressure lately, and it helps me unwind with a few drinks after work.

Pastor: It does sound like you're worrying about something, Jim. Is it something you can discuss with me?

Without going any farther with the conversation between the pastor and Jim Jeffries, it is important to consider how the pastor's knowledge, presence, and guidance may be involved in this situation. The pastor's first responsibility as a carer is to ask about the behavior that he has observed. His inclination may be to ignore what he has seen and simply talk about the church job to be done. It is important that the pastor be firmly present, talk straight, and not deny the problem as Jim is likely to do.

After being up front in recognizing Jim's drinking behavior, the pastor's second responsibility is to move away from talking about the drinking. Jim can avoid dealing with himself by talking about his drinking or not drinking and thus avoid touching on whatever is painful in his life story. It is important that the pastor not get sucked into that. Instead, he asks Jim about his feelings and whether or not he can talk about whatever is bothering him. The pastor begins with something with which he is familiar—people's feelings of hurt. He is familiar with that from his ministry in times of grief and illness. If Jim is able to share himself and his feelings and use the relationship with the pastor in a personal way, it may indicate that he can address some of the pain in his life without alcohol or the treatment of his addiction.

In thinking about the problem, the pastor might wonder about the pain in Jim's present family and his family of origin. He should be open to Jim's talking about those family issues, but needs to be careful with any "poor old Jim" feelings he finds stirring. He should also, as has already been noted, avoid getting involved in a lengthy discussion of Jim's drinking behavior, his drinking or stopping drinking. If that is the way Jim continues to present himself and his problems, the pastor needs to know that a referral to an addiction specialist is required without delay. If he can talk about the more relational issues in his life, referral for treatment of substance abuse may be delayed or possibly avoided.

In the more likely case, if the pastor's question about Jim's worry is met with denial of any problem, blame of others, the work situation, and so on, then the pastor should know that Jim's abusive behavior toward himself—his drinking—has been substituted for awareness of his feelings, and the addictive process must be addressed first. Certainly, this is oversimplifying a complex issue, but what the pastor needs to know is whether or not he or she can lead from the familiar point of working with human hurt. If not, it is important to begin the process of trying to refer Jim to the best available community resource for dealing with his problem.

The word "begin" is used here because the process will likely take some time. The pastor will probably want to tell Jim that he is concerned about his drinking and let Jim know that he intends to share that concern with Jim's wife, Jean. Then the pastor will repeat the process of seeing where Jean is with her feelings and consider referral for her to a group, such as Al-Anon, for family members of abusers. The pastor needs to know about the kind of denial that is so prominent in abusing families, be firm in his response, and be ready to act in referring Jim for treatment.

Is Jim Jeffries abuse of self with alcohol sin or sickness? The church has sometimes held a rigid, oversimplified view that understood the abuse of self through addiction as caused by personal failings that had formed into a stubborn, sinful pattern of behavior. The cure for such behavior was understood to be the same as for all other sins: confession of sin and conversion to a new life of faith. James B. Nelson, a theological ethicist and recovering alcoholic, describes the view of addiction as simply stubborn, sinful behavior as one end of a continuum that addresses the question of whether addiction is disease or sin.[1] At the other end of this continuum is the view that addiction is purely a disease and that sin is not a factor in it.

In the middle of the sin or disease continuum are three other views: (1) addiction begins as sin (in the decision to drink) and later becomes a disease; (2) addiction is sin and disease all mixed together (Although Alcoholics Anonymous does not use the word "sin," its position seems closest to this one.); and (3) addiction is a disease resulting from sin, but the sin is outside the responsibility of the addicted person. (Addiction results from social sin—abusive family systems, racism, sexism, poverty, and the drug-soaked culture that we all live in. The addict is largely a victim.) What is important is that the pastor have some idea about what his or her own view on this issue is.

What is more important is that the pastor know what resources for treatment are available in his or her community. It can be very helpful for pastors to have some direct knowledge of the A.A. and other twelve-step groups that are available. Or if there is a for-profit treatment facility in the community, the pastor should know something about that facility's practices. Do its ethics balance appropriately with its need for patients? What other community resources are available, such as psychologists and psychiatrists who are knowledgeable about groups for addiction related problems? If the pastor is to refer as an appropriate expression of care, he or she needs to know to what and to whom he or she is referring. This will be discussed further in the chapter on pastoral counseling.

Abuse of Others

Awareness of physical, emotional, and sexual abuse as a problem for pastoral care is a relatively recent phenomenon. Secrecy about such abuse has been strongly supported by the power of shame and has made exposure of the problem particularly difficult. Surely, anything so shameful could not possibly be true. Nevertheless, child sexual abuse, for one example, has a long history in American society. Until the ascendancy of psychology in the twentieth century, however, Americans failed to identify child victims of sexual abuse because such crimes were hidden. Disbelief that such behavior occurred and distrust of young victims marked the early legal opinions on the subject. Moreover, in the case of child victims, if pregnancy could not result, the sexual act was not perceived as a concern of the law. On the other hand, child victims were viewed as accomplices who required corroboration in some form, preferably a confession by the defendant. If family members continued to stand by the accused, it was virtually impossible to convict the perpetrator.

A pastor may encounter a situation something like this. A young mother, Margaret Miller, stops pastor Ellen Edwards in the church hallway. Margaret appears to have been crying. Ellen invites Margaret into her office and asks:

> **Pastor:** Those tears look like painful ones, Margaret. Do you feel like telling me what they are about?

> **Margaret:** I don't know whether I can or not. I'm so ashamed. I suppose I should be angry, but I just feel betrayed and ashamed.

> **Pastor:** Shame is terribly difficult to deal with, but it might help if you could tell me something about what's going on.

> **Mary:** It's Mike, my husband. I have just discovered that he's been exposing himself sexually to our seven-year-old daughter. It's awful! I don't think any more than that has happened, but I don't know for sure.

How does the pastor respond to Ms. Miller's pain? What does she need to know, to be, and to do? She responds first by thinking about it. Her response might be essentially the same as Margaret Miller's—"it's awful"—but she can be more helpful if she can avoid letting her feelings get in the way of Margaret expressing hers. She also needs to have a way of thinking about the problem and encouraging Margaret to think about it before she acts. Moreover, like the pastor of Jim Jeffries, Pastor Edwards also needs to lead from strength. She knows about pain from situations of illness and grief and first must deal with Margaret Miller's feelings, and perhaps her own, particularly if she is unusually shocked by what she has heard. Ms. Miller needs to tell the story as she knows it in the context of a trusting relationship, and Pastor Edwards needs to be fully present to Margaret's pain. She is aware that shame is terribly difficult to deal with, but she also knows that beginning to address it rather than attempting to hide it can help.

Although dealing with some of Margaret's feelings comes first and is important, the pastor needs to know and do a number of other things. In preparation for an event such as this one, she needs to have consulted with a lawyer about the abuse laws in her state and what is necessary for addressing the abuse when it occurs within the family and outside it. Both she and Jim Jeffries's pastor should have a subcommittee of the church governing board that is responsible for the church's care and counseling ministry. That committee should, among other things on its agenda, have discussed legal and ethical responsibilities of the pastor and church in the case of reported abuse. If pastors are required by state law to report cases of alleged abuse, how is that to be done and to what person or agency? The responsibilities and function of such a committee will be discussed further in the chapter on pastoral counseling.

As a part of her pastoral concern to respond to her parishioner's feelings the pastor needs to inform Margaret of legal requirements about reporting alleged abuse. This limit on the pastor's ability to maintain confidentiality should be made clear as soon as she hears of any kind of situation of abuse. The pastor also needs to find out what Margaret has done with her discovery of the abuse and what she wants to do. Depending somewhat on the circumstances, Margaret may need to talk with her pediatrician and use that resource for any other referral for her daughter. Pastor Edwards needs to help Margaret begin to evaluate the possibility of further abuse and to consider where she is with her husband and some of the possible courses of action she may take. Thus, in order to help, the pastor needs to know something about abuse, be present to Margaret in a dependable trustworthy relationship, and be ready to guide and support any appropriate action that Margaret takes.

Unless there is clear danger of immediate further abuse, she should not take any precipitous action. The pastor works to stabilize the situation and yet work with all deliberate speed. Depending on her relationship with Margaret's husband, the pastor will consider discussing the situation with him alone or with the couple. Prior to that interview, if at all possible, she should make use of a consultant, someone who can help her assess her responsibilities and possible action that should be taken in the situation. Again, this discussion risks oversimplification and is dealing with a case that may be somewhat simpler to deal with than those that many pastors have to face. Most important is that pastors not work in isolation and that they have a plan in place for dealing with pastoral events such as this.

One of the things a pastor needs to have in order to minister to persons who seek help for abuse of themselves or of others is a way of thinking about the problem. One of the ways to interpret abuse from a theological perspective is as failure to care and the shame that results. The human being is pictured as one who abuses or who may abuse what has been given into his or her care, hiding and denying what he or she has done. And it is this condition that the pastor must address in a situation of abuse either of self or of others. Psychologically, the abuse of self or others is most likely related to some significant failure in caring by the abuser's earliest caretakers. Abusers of self or others attempt to deal with the shame of having not received what they sought in their early relationships with those who cared for then by abusing other relationships or turning their shame inward in the form of rage toward themselves for their inadequacy and weakness. Abusers may try to hide their shame in substance abuse or deny it by violating the boundaries of others in a futile attempt to get something that will make them feel satisfied, or let others repeatedly violate their boundaries. An abused person also experiences shame, a misplaced shame that sometimes protects the abuser. Shame also proceeds from being too weak to prevent the abuse.

The value of this kind of psychological theory is that it is based in a relational understanding of human beings that resonates with a classical or biblical view. Moreover, it provides a way of thinking about how the refusal to care or the failure to care may develop. Although the pastor in a parish situation will not usually be involved in the treatment of an addicted or abused person, in his or her relationships with that person he or she should be aware of the fragility of the abused person's self-esteem. Though he or she is not treating the person's addiction or abuse, the pastor can offer an informal caring relationship in which the addicted or abused person can recover some of his or her self-esteem.

In recent years, health professionals have identified a pattern of behavior adopted by child victims of sexual abuse and called it "child abuse accommodation syndrome." The syndrome is composed of five elements: (1) secrecy, which defines the circumstance in which the sexual abuse occurs; (2) helplessness, which defines the condition in which children are often given permission to avoid the attention of strangers, but are required to be obedient and affectionate with adults entrusted with their care; (3) entrapment and accommodation, which defines the child's initial response to sexual assault. Because the child cannot escape or disclose the assaults without destroying the family and his or her security, he or she learns to accept the situation in order to survive; (4) delayed, unconvincing disclosure will often be the child's response in a family when there is conflict between parental authorities; and (5) retraction of his or her disclosure is likely to follow if the assailant abandons the child, calls the child a liar, or if the child's mother becomes hysterical or does not believe him or her.[2]

The thing that has been most surprising to pastors and other counselors who have been told stories of sexual abuse is how the mother tolerated the abuse or could not believe that it was happening because of her conscious or unconscious awareness of her own or her family's vulnerability if she attempted to stop the abuse. She was aware that she and her children might be turned out without any means of financial support—that their overall life situation might be worse than if nothing was done.

Marie Fortune addresses pastors with practical guidelines for what to know, to be, and to do about abuse. First of all, she says, you, the pastor, need to be aware of your own comfort level with the issues of sexual assault, abuse, and sexuality. Everyone has biases and prejudices, and certain types of people with whom we do not work well; therefore do not hesitate to refer people with whom you can't work so that they may get help from a colleague.

Second, when you observe symptoms or suspect abuse, ask. Pastors are often reluctant to ask about things like abuse, suicidal feelings, or rape, apparently feeling that they should somehow know these things instinctively. It is important to deal with the shame, fear, and embarrassment that may prevent us asking directly for the information we need to help us help those within our pastoral care.

Third, make a habit of routinely including questions about possible experiences of sexual violence early in any pastoral counseling interviews. Again, it is easy to avoid such topics, but the fact that we have avoided them is part of the problem. Premarital counseling interviews may reveal some of the ways that a couple deals with conflict and the potential for abuse. Personal interviews with confirmands or other occasions of speaking with young people alone may provide opportunities to hear stories of abuse.

Should this happen, the pastor should ask if the young person has been to a rape crisis center or other source of aid. If he or she has not, find out if he or she wishes to contact someone who deals regularly with abuse or wishes to talk with you further about it. Respect his or her decision if he or she is not ready, but let him or her know that you, or other resources, are available.

Fourth, make every effort to ask your questions in a matter-of-fact, normal, respectful tone of voice. Your calmness and professional attitude can ease the feelings of shame and secrecy and may make disclosure possible at some future time. For example, "A lot of people have experienced a situation in which someone has abused or assaulted them. Has that ever happened to you?"

Fifth, the pastor needs to be aware of and to use community resources for dealing with sexual abuse. Knowing where and how to refer is important. The pastor may also consider taking some in-depth training in dealing with abuse or calling a crisis or counseling center for advice when he or she needs consultation and guidance.[3]

In working therapeutically with perpetrators of boundary violations, James N. Poling has noted that one of the most difficult issues for these persons is setting limits and appropriate boundaries. "It is obvious," he says, "that a man who molests a child does not know how to set limits on his own destructive behaviors, and does not respect the boundaries that other persons need in order to survive."[4] In their work with male adult sex offenders, family therapists Merle Fossum and Marilyn Mason found that many of these men had been deprived of nurturing touch in their childhood experiences. "What they had been denied, they had later taken; in the process they ended up violating others' boundaries. The denied or invaded touch resulted in that victim's 'taking' safe touch from some vulnerable young person."[5] Pastors need to understand the shame and how it contributes to abuse because that can allow them to act rather than just to react to what appears to be irrational and shameless behavior on the part of the abuser. Again, the legal requirement for reporting sexual abuse varies from state to state. The minister needs to know the law in his or her state and have that interpreted for him or her from a legal perspective. He or she also needs to sort out his or her own understanding of confidentiality and then gain some knowledge of how the law of that particular state has been recently interpreted.[6]

84

The recent literature on the pastoral care of women has been helpful in increasing awareness of the reality of male abuse of the less powerful. This kind of failure to care is not confined to individuals, but is expressed in societal structures as well. It is important for pastors to recognize that those in power tend to view their own behavior as the norm for everyone. A gender, race, or class that is in power tends to hold on to that power by not being able to see things any other way or by a failure to experience shame over the way things are. This is a reality, underscored by a theological view of sin, that may be seen in attitudes that encourage abuse of children, women, or other races and classes. Good pastoral care of victims requires that pastors examine their premises and prejudices about violence and about sexuality, their life experience and deepest feelings about women and men, and their beliefs about parents and children and family life.[7]

Pastors need to be aware of the kind of victim blaming that has gone on even in the church, particularly in its understanding of forgiveness. The church and its leaders have often been prone to encourage abused persons to forgive their abusers even in cases when forgiveness would involve denial of the anger necessary for healing. Marie Fortune and others have suggested that there are times when pastoral care clearly calls for anger rather than forgiveness. Pastors need to know that:

1. Forgiveness is not forgetting. We cannot forget, nor should we, because those experiences, even the pain they caused, have a great deal to teach us.

2. Forgiveness is not condoning. We are not saying that what was done to us was acceptable or "not so bad."

3. Forgiveness is not absolving those who have hurt us of all responsibility for their actions. They are still responsible for what they did and must deal with it themselves.

4. Forgiveness is not a form of self-sacrifice or swallowing our true feelings and playing the martyr.

5. Perhaps most important, forgiveness is not a clear-cut, one-time decision. We can't simply decide that today we are going to forgive. If it happens, it happens as a result of confronting painful past experiences and healing of old wounds.

What, then, is forgiveness?

1. It is a discovery, the by-product of an ongoing healing process. Failure to forgive is not a failure of will but happens because wounds have not yet healed.

2. Rather than being something we do, forgiveness is something that happens as a sign of positive self-esteem, when we are no longer building our identity around something that happened in the past. Our injuries are just a part of who we are, not all of us.

3. It is recognizing that we no longer need our hatred and resentments and no longer need to punish the people who hurt us, wanting them to suffer as much as we did.

4. Realizing that punishing them does not heal us, forgiveness is putting to better use the energy once consumed by rage and resentment and moving on with life.

Finally, because of the power differential between the participants and the resulting possibility of shame, there is the potential for abuse in the pastoral relationship itself. Anyone who has done a great deal of hospital visitation has probably experienced something like this. The pastor visits and the patient "opens up" to the pastor about some of his worries and concerns. Afterward, the pastor goes away feeling as if he or she has done well, established trust with the patient and is on the way to a significant pastoral relationship. On the next visit, however, the pastor is surprised to find that the patient acts as if he hardly knows the pastor. In contrast to the "open" way the patient related before, today he seems closed and distant.

The pastor leaves this second visit feeling confused. If he or she were more aware of the function of shame in relationships where people "open up," he or she would not be too surprised. Probably, without being aware of it, the pastor encouraged the patient to share more of himself than he was ready to share. On the next visit the pastor should be more aware of the patient's need to protect himself from the shame of too much openness. Most important is the pastor's being aware that persons who acknowledge their need for help are more than likely experiencing some shame because of needing that help. One of the pastor's major responsibilities is seeing to it that he or she is not abusive in his or her pastoral relationships.[8]

Summary and Reflection

The character of the care described in this chapter has been somewhat different. Hearing and remembering goes beyond the present to the pattern revealed by the past, and the care of the pastor is expressed by remembering and confronting the abuser or the abused person with the fact that this has happened before and that the abuse is not to be minimized and denied. It must be addressed and addressed now or even more serious consequences will result. The pastor needs to have knowledge about addiction and abuse, knowledge of addiction groups and other treatment options, knowledge of shelters for the abused, of state laws for reporting abuse, and of persons within and outside the church who can work with the pastor in addressing situations of abuse. There is a great deal that needs to be known and, often, to be done. Nevertheless, the pastor's presence continues to be an essential part of pastoral wisdom, even though in dealing with abuse of self and others, knowledge and guidance seem to be the important requirements. Although there is greater dependence on help from persons and agencies other than the pastor, the pastor's presence in the referral process helps maintain a significant connection between the abused and the abuser with a faith community. Often the shame involved in abuse prevents reconnection with the community that the pastor represents. Nevertheless, a pastor's caring presence makes reconnection with another faith community much more likely.

CHAPTER 7

Care of Marriage and Family

God setteth the solitary in families. —Psalm 68:6 KJV

W hat kind of wisdom does a pastor need in order to care for a family in crisis? How does a pastor with little or no training in marriage and family counseling assist members of his or her parish or other persons who may have turned to him or her for help? Again, knowledge, presence, and guidance are what is necessary, but in response to family issues they appear in different ways. Pastoral care for more than one person involves a different kind of listening, a different kind of hearing and remembering. It is more structured and requires knowledge of a system of relationships as well as hearing and remembering an individual's story. Although pastors need to be reminded that they are not family therapists and are not expected to cure, they also need to be reminded that they can minister to families by making use of many of the things that they already know about pastoral care. The pastor's task is not to *cure* but to provide a structure in which he or she can convey his or her *care* and ability to communicate with each member of the family in the presence of the other members.

The Family and Care of Our Generations

What kind of knowledge is needed in order to care for marriage and the family? First of all, the pastor needs to have a way of thinking about families and how they should function. If one understands the Hebrew word in Genesis 1:28 that has traditionally been translated "have dominion over" as "care for" or "take responsibility for" the earth and all that is in it, knowledge about what the family should be can begin there. Men and women have, from the very beginning, been given the vocation of caring for the earth and thus for themselves and others. This means caring for oneself as an individual person and caring for the significant relationships in one's life. We are called, as the great commandment also reminds us, to love both self and other.

In carrying out this responsibility, the Bible, particularly the Old Testament, reminds us that we are not just individuals. We are persons who are a part of generations. Some of the most difficult public reading of the Bible comes in the recital of generations. "These are the generations of Abraham, Isaac, and Jacob. . . ." This is dull prose, but it is an important extension of the commandment to honor our parents. It places us among the generations of our family and reminds us of who we are. We are connected to each other, and that is a profound ethical responsibility. To be a human being is to care for those who have come before and for those who come after us, as well as to care for ourselves and our partner in marriage. One of the things that marriage therapists have learned in doing therapy with couples is that you cannot build and sustain a marriage by only caring for your own generation. It requires the care of all three—the generation of which one is a part and shares with one's spouse, the generation that came before one and the generation that comes after one. Certainly, there are other ways to think about how the family needs to function, but this way is grounded in a theological-ethical understanding of humanity, its responsibilities, and what Christian ministry attempts to support. Pastoral presence and guidance involves reminding couples of this.

Communicating Generational Care

Probably the first opportunity of communicating this kind of view of the family comes in premarital consultation. Pastors who choose to do little or no work with troubled families do deal with the way that marriages function in their premarital consultation with couples. For most pastors there are at least two meetings with the couple prior to the wedding rehearsal and ceremony. One session is needed for the pastor to get acquainted with the couple as adults who have made an important decision about their lives. He needs to know that what they have in mind for a marriage service fits with the view of marriage of the Christian community that the pastor represents. If it does not, and if discussion and negotiation does not change their view, then it is not likely that the pastor can perform the marriage service for them.

A second session is needed to fulfill three purposes: to further the pastor's understanding of the couple and where they are in their lives; to interpret more to them of the meaning of the wedding ritual that will be used; and to develop some sort of relationship between the couple and the pastor and church. The importance of this last purpose is that it can pave the way for future pastoral care with this pastor or, more likely, another pastor. One way of thinking about what a premarital consultation can do is that it provides an interpretive bridge between the couple's present life situation, their families of origin, and the way that the church has historically offered blessing to a marriage.

If a pastor meets with a premarital couple for more than wedding preparation, there is more opportunity to convey a generational understanding of the family. Most couples who meet with pastors prior to a marriage are not particularly interested in receiving guidance about their own relationship. They are most often motivated primarily by romantic love and are bent on carrying out their decision to marry without anyone else raising questions about it. What can be done quite profitably, however, is encouraging the couple to look at the marital relationships in the prior generation of their families. With the help of the pastor, they are able to surface some of their assumptions about what marriage is and talk about what that might mean for maintaining their own marriage.

With the biblical vocation to care in mind, the pastor can ask couples to look at the way that the various members of their families cared for each other. What negative and positive images of how couples care for each other were expressed in the marriage of their prior generation? Raising a question like this is not simply

91

gathering information for information's sake but enabling a couple to see how influential the parental generation is in their relationship to each other. This can be done through a discussion of family stories, myths, and traditions as well as examining the roles of various family members and the explicit and implicit rules for family behavior in the respective families. The point is to bring into the open the couple's assumptions about what marriage is and should be, and to remind them that their generations are a part of their marriage.

Usually, a discussion of the prior generation's marriages and their customs helps couples discuss the future as well as the past. The pastor may ask, "What do you envision your family to be like in three years, seven, or ten years?" "Will you have children?" Both the physical fact and the symbolic meaning of having children expresses most clearly the commitment to care for and to invest in the future. "How have you thought of contributing to the future generation if you do not have children of your own?" Whatever the result of the couple's decision about whether to have children, there appears to be a powerful human need in most of us to contribute in some way to the future generation. That need and responsibility should be recognized and discussed in premarital consultation.

Caring for One's Own Generation

The theme of care in the pastor's knowledge about marriage and the family is supported by some important social-psychological views of marriage. Three of those theories are discussed here. Family therapists Lyman and Adele Wynne say that intimacy in the marriage relationship is built on four things: (1) attachment and caregiving, the prototype for which is the parent-child relationship; (2) a communicating process in which there is an exchange of meanings and messages; (3) joint problem solving and the sharing of everyday tasks; and (4) mutuality, understood as the integration of the first three processes into an enduring pattern of relatedness. What the Wynnes are saying is that until attachment and caregiving are incorporated into a relationship, that relationship is not likely to become enduring and reliable.[1]

Similar to the Wynnes' second point about the importance of sharing meanings and messages, another social theorist, Peter Berger, speaks of marriage in terms of persons developing a common world of meaning. He "takes a text" from the book of Genesis and argues that its picture of God's giving to humankind the task of naming the animals is symbolic of the essentially human task of ordering the world in meaningful relationship to oneself. Some of this can be seen in children when they begin to talk and name things in order to understand where they belong. This should take place on a different level with adults. The reality of our personal world is sustained through conversation with significant others. Berger says that the plausibility and stability of the world, as socially defined, is dependent on the strength and continuity of significant relationships in which conversation about this world can be continually carried on. Couples must work at this in order to develop and maintain their marriage. The closeness and intimacy in a marriage relationship grows out of the construction of a common world of meaning through conversation. [2]

These ways of thinking about the theme of care within one's own generation can be helpful to a pastor in understanding what is or is not going on in a marriage. Another important way of thinking about marriage involves the question so often voiced in one way or another in a marriage consultation, "How can I be myself when I am in relationship to another person?" Psychological health always involves the ability to maintain one's self in relationships, particularly those involving intimacy and closeness. The late Tom Malone and his son Pat, both psychiatrists, have addressed the balance of care of self and care of the other by contrasting the meanings of these terms.[3]

As a marriage deteriorates, couples find that they don't have enough of either closeness or intimacy. Closeness is the experience in which one is more aware of the other person than of oneself. One is more aware of another's needs than one's own. It can be a wonderful experience of care for the partner giving and the one receiving. At best, the giving and receiving is balanced between the partners. Taking care of another, however, is almost always the opposite of caring for them. The Malones—as have many others— distinguish between care and caretaking. Caring enhances and enlivens both persons; taking care of diminishes both. Taking care of the other is too much like providing a service rather than offering a relationship. It is a bit like Martha in the New Testament story of Mary and Martha, who complained to Jesus about her sister not helping her with the work around the house (Luke 10:40). Nevertheless, caring for the needs of the other as a means of closeness is one of the essentials of a good marriage.

In contrast to closeness, a relationship is intimate when a couple is together and each is more aware of themselves than they are aware of the other person in the relationship. Intimacy makes each person feel more intense and alive while in the presence of the significant other. It is not that in intimate experience you are only aware of yourself and not the other. Rather, it is that in the experience of intimacy you are aware of yourself as being more of who you are when you are in that relationship than when you are separated from it.

That kind of experience of oneself is profoundly sexual, but not necessarily genital. The essence of intimacy is the intense self-awareness that one has in the immediate presence of another person to whom one is significantly related. This is why intimacy is so energizing. It changes the balances of care of self and care of the other in a way that supports the deeper dimensions of love. Loving oneself and loving the other person in the relationship come together. Marriages are maintained and strengthened by developing the ability to be both close and intimate. Both closeness (awareness and response to the need of the other) and intimacy (experiencing oneself most fully when in the presence of the other) deepen the capacity to care for self and one another in all the generations for whom one cares.

Helping Families Discover How They Care: More Thinking About It

What should happen when a pastor is confronted with a marriage or family crisis that calls for her care? Certainly she needs to have some of the knowledge we have discussed, but she also needs to be able to offer presence and guidance that are a part of all pastoral care. A pastor who recognizes that she is not a marriage and family therapist and does not try to be one can assist persons in caring for their marriages and families by helping them discover how they are caring for themselves, for the relationships in their own generation, and for the generations before and after them. Pastoral wisdom includes the knowledge that tensions involved in the care of one's generations and care for self and for one's significant other are always taking place in families. The pastor who has understood some of this is better able to engage a family in dialogue about their balances of care. That dialogue can in most cases help move the family in the direction of a more appropriate balance of care between self and other and between self and one's generations.

This balance of care takes place, first of all, by thinking whole family or the family system—the way family members are related—not just about the one who has made the pastor aware of the problem. Only one member of the family may have voiced the family's pain, and because it is more familiar and comfortable to talk with one person than more than one, the pastor will be tempted to respond to the marital or family crisis responding only to one family member. The pastor's responsibility, however, is to care for the whole family and if the family is a member of the faith community that the pastor represents and serves, the pastor has already been given permission to care actively for each member of the family system. If the family is not a member of that community, the pastor has probably been consulted at least partially because of what he or she represents. Thus, he or she has been given some authority to care and to structure the situation of care.

What a Pastor Can Do in Caring for Marriage and the Family

In terms of what should actually be done, the pastor's first task is to get the family together for a family consultation. In the majority of the situations with which the pastor finds himself or herself involved, "getting the family together" means making every possible effort to see the marital couple together in the first interview and avoiding situations in which the person seeking help talks about his or her spouse or other family members without those persons being present. A number of calls that a pastor receives have to do with concerns about a marriage. If the pastor is not careful, responding to the call for help of one member of a marriage relationship can be competitive with rather than supportive of the marriage; therefore a structuring conversation such as the following can be quite important.

Parishioner: Reverend Smith, this is Joyce Jones. I would like to come in and talk to you.

Pastor: Are you free to tell me a little of what it's about over the phone?

Parishioner: I'd rather not. I'm at the office, and this is not a good place to talk. Do you have any time this week?

Pastor: My usual practice is to see married persons together with their spouse. My experience has been that both members of a marriage should be present the first time I see a married person. It helps me to understand the situation better from each person's point of view.

Parishioner: I would like that, but there are some things that it would be easier for me to talk about without my husband there, and it would also be hard for him to get off from work.

Pastor: I've discovered that, for me at least, it's more important to see something of the relationship the first time I meet with someone than it is to hear the things that are difficult to talk about together. Let me ask you to do this. Talk with your husband. Ask him to come with you the first time, and see what he says.

Parishioner: *(Apparently somewhat irritated)* I already know what he'll say. He won't come.

Pastor: I know that you probably do know what he'll say, but I encourage you to try it anyway. Tell him that it's just my way of working with families, and maybe he will understand. Call me back tomorrow and tell me what he said.

Parishioner: Well, all right, but I already know what will happen.

Pastor: I'll look forward to hearing about it tomorrow.

It is difficult to overemphasize the importance of this kind of preliminary conversation. The pastor indicates early in the call that he wants Ms. Jones's spouse to know who he is and how he works. If she does decide to come in, their relationship is not going to be secretive. In fact, he attempts to make it clear that relationships are more important than secrets anyway.

The pastor takes a strong stand in structuring the first interview. In doing so, he is attempting to illustrate the importance of talking with one's significant other rather than assuming what he or she will say. This kind of firm structuring is also important in setting up the best conditions under which a pastoral counseling interview can take place. If these conditions are clear and firm, then the counselees are more likely to feel that the pastoral counselor knows what he or she is doing, even though they may not like all of it. A firm structure for counseling makes it more likely for the couple to believe that something useful is going to happen than with counseling that begins with an "anything goes" kind of philosophy.

The pastor who has gathered family members into his or her office or other suitable place for a consultation needs to remember that whatever he or she may have learned about the importance of presence or "being with" still holds. It is usually true, however, that family members are so strongly related to each other that the pastor will have to be much more active than in individual care in order to be with the individual members when they are in one another's presence. Pastoral care of a couple or larger family group involves more active structuring and guidance in the communication process. A pastor who is working with an individual can afford to be more passive and focus his or her care on listening. When a pastor works with more than one person, although being with and listening are never negated, he or she needs to be much more active in structuring the interview. This is particularly true for the relatively untrained pastor: the less training, the more structure. It may be more helpful to think of such a family meeting like this as a consultation rather than family counseling. The pastoral family interview may be likened to a classroom in which the teacher is clearly in charge, where he or she is encouraging each member of the class to talk and at the same time using his or her authority to encourage the others to listen.

When the family has been gathered, the basic method of the family care consultation is talking individually with each member of the family in the presence of the others. This is often not easy to do. Various members of the family may try to dominate the interview or keep silent. The pastor's concern is that the voice of each family member is heard by the pastor and the family members themselves. This respects the commitment and loyalties that the family members have, but at the same time affirms their separation and individuality. It illustrates the balance of care between self and others and the concern for all of the generations of the family.

Other than the central concern with the balance of care in the family, the most important assumption for the pastor to hold in the process of engaging the family is that it is the whole family that is troubled, not just one of the members. It is the whole family's behavior that is a problem or that causes pain. It is the whole family or both members of the couple that are out of balance. If this assumption is undermined, the ineffective family pattern will more than likely be reconfirmed rather than have the possibility of being changed.

The way the pastor structures a situation in which the whole family or as many as possible are together and the questions or comments that he or she makes during the process of the interview is often referred to as an intervention. Intervention is a useful concept because of its literal meaning, "coming between." The pastor in his or her dialogue is, in fact, moving in between or among the relationships within the family system. The intervention is not a cure for what is dysfunctional in the family, but it can help change the pattern of relationships within the family. The family acts differently when there is a nonfamily member in their midst. In the case of a pastoral family interview the purpose of the intervention is to help the family become more aware of how they usually relate to one another. If they can see a pattern, they will have a choice to make changes in it.

The pastor begins the consultation by asking a question like this: "What's not working in the family?" Or the pastor may begin the interview by sharing his or her first awareness of the problem, saying something like: "George spoke to me after church last Sunday and said that the family was experiencing a lot of tension, and I wanted the whole family to get together and see if my talking about it with you would help." (Note that the pastor does not present the problem as it was presented to him, but redefines it as a family problem in the first statement he or she makes. If the initial statement begins to reinterpret what is going on as belonging to the family, something useful will have already been offered to the family.)

To whom is the first question to the family addressed? Family therapists differ in their approaches, although there is some unanimity that the identified patient or problem should not be addressed first in order that the concept of family pain rather than individual problem can be conveyed. The statement or question about the family pain or problem may be addressed to the whole family to see who will respond first. It may be addressed to one family member, either the one with most concern about the family's getting some help or, perhaps, to the one who seems least concerned or involved. With the latter approach there is more likelihood that what is happening in the whole family will be addressed, rather than the presenting problem that has been identified by the most concerned family member.

As he has done in the pastoral care of individuals dealing with other human problems, the pastor looks for and responds to the pain of each person within the system but not so much that he or she loses touch with what else seems to be going on with the other members of the family. Although the pastor is an outsider to the family system, he or she can in effect be an insider to the individuals within it by his or her sensitivity to the feelings of family members. What is perhaps most important is that the pastor actively structure the dialogue so that it takes place between the family member and the pastor. Particularly for a pastor with limited training, this is the only way that he or she can maintain control of the interview and take at least some steps to break up the dysfunctional pattern of interaction and communication within the family.

A useful way of structuring a pastoral family interview is to raise the same question with each member of the family successively and attempt to have a similar dialogue with each on the same question or issue. As was suggested earlier, the first question to each family member has to do with the family pain. The second question can be how long each family member has been aware of the pain and his or her observations of how it affects each member. A third question may be asking from each member what he or she thinks should be done to deal with the family's problem.

Although only three specific questions or interventions have been mentioned here, many things go on in the process of making them. Some concepts used for describing families in the literature of family therapy may be useful in the process. Thus some of what may happen can be interpreted as an increased awareness of family roles, boundaries between persons and generations, secrets, customs, patterns of communication, rules, and so on. For the relatively untrained pastor, however, the major concepts he or she employs can be the balances of care: how the family members are dealing with relationships to their generations and how they are balancing needs for closeness and needs for the experience of being a unique individual. Interpreting to the family what the pastor observes about these issues is almost always useful in helping family members become aware of things that they had taken for granted. The assumption here is that awareness of the way things are now makes change possible. Experiencing the pastor as one who does not see the family in the same way the family does suggests that there are alternative ways of being and understanding.

It is most important for the pastor to remember what he or she already has some experience with—responding to the pain of individuals by letting them know that they are heard and will be remembered. The difference with couple or family consultation, however, should be stated again. In order to hear and remember, the pastor has to be very active in structuring so that one voice can be heard at a time and that that voice can also be effectively heard by others who are present. This does not "cure" the family or necessarily "solve" the presenting problem, but it may make it possible for the family to begin to change itself.

This discussion of pastoral family intervention is applicable to meetings both with couples and with parents and children. In meeting only with a couple, however, several other things need to be emphasized. In couples interviews the pastor may need to be even more active in structuring the dialogue so that it takes place primarily between the pastor and each member of the couple in turn. The questions to the couple may be the same or similar to those used in a family interview. They should deal with the problem as each person, in turn, sees it. How long has the problem been going on? What are each person's hopes or plans for changing the situation? Perhaps the most important thing in a couples' interview with a pastor is the opportunity for each person to share his or her pain in the situation with a caring person, the pastor, while the spouse listens to what is being said. Much of this may have been said to the spouse before, but it is quite often heard in a different way when it is said to another. It is like overhearing something that one didn't expect to hear and becoming aware of it in a different way. The interview should be structured so that this can take place.

Throughout the process of pastoral consultation with a couple or family it is important to recall again that one's worth as a pastoral carer depends on caring, not curing. Any healing that occurs is more gift than an accomplishment. Pastoral intervention almost inevitably allows the family to experience things differently, and in relation to a caring pastor representing a caring community, feel enough freedom and support to try something new. Even if that does not happen, there can be real satisfaction for family members in knowing that the pastor has tried to understand what is going on rather than just assuming that someone is to blame for it.

Summary and Reflection

The character of the care described in this chapter is more like that in the chapter on abuse than the care discussed in the first five chapters. Although pastoral presence continues to be important, there has been a stronger emphasis on knowing and doing. The pastor needs to have a way of thinking about marriage and family that builds on what he or she already knows—hearing, remembering, and responding to individuals in pain. What is also needed for the care of the family, however, is the ability to think and respond to the couple or family system. It is important not to disrespect the marriage or family by responding only to the individual who expresses the pain in the system.

Caring for marriage and the family more often than not requires referral to an experienced therapist who has adequate training to address the family problem. (More will be said about referral in the chapter that follows.) The pastor's informed response to the family's pain, however, can make any referral much more effective. What is important to emphasize here is that if the pastor can consult with the family without thinking of himself or herself as a family therapist, he or she can contribute significantly to the way that the family members care for each other and respond to a marriage and family therapist.

As was the case in responding to situations of abuse, care of the family involves a more assertive and active pastoral stance. The pastor must be a strong guide. The guidance is usually not in telling the family members how to live their lives, but in guiding them by structuring their getting together and the way they speak and attempt to hear each other as family members. Again the pastor's task is not primarily to solve a family problem, but to help family members become aware of how, as children of God, created in and for relationship, they balance their care for themselves and for their generations.

CHAPTER 8

Pastoral Counseling

"Then pay attention to how you listen." —Luke 8:18*a*

Pastoral counseling is not a ministry that stands alone. It is a part of the larger caring ministry of the congregation. Pastoral counseling is the type of pastoral care in which the receiver of care has in some way initiated the pastoral conversation and directly or indirectly asked for help. Like all pastoral care it requires the pastor's knowledge, presence, and guidance. How a pastor's counseling is different from counseling provided by other counselors in the community has more to do with the person and accountability of the pastor than with the methods adopted for the counseling. The primary criterion for method is that it is consistent with what ministry is and with what persons and relationships are understood to be within the context of Christian faith.

Pastoral Counseling, a Ministry of the Church

Because the counseling that a pastor does is a part of his or her church's ministry of pastoral care, the parish minister has an important accountability to that community of faith for the counseling that he or she does. Pastoral counseling in a parish situation requires that the community, not the pastor alone, be responsible for it. The parish minister's accountability for his or her counseling is an important issue because far too many pastors carry out their pastoral counseling in secret. Too often there is no group within the church that knows how much and what kind of counseling the pastor is doing and what percentage his or her ministry is devoted to this activity.

The confidentiality that is so important in any kind of counseling does not have to be compromised by the pastor's reporting regularly to a duly authorized committee of the church. The church needs to know through this committee how much of the pastor's time is spent in this way, any money received for these services or given away to persons in need, the types of situations that he may be dealing with, the consultation about his counseling that he is receiving and from whom he is receiving it. It is also important for the committee to know how much of the pastor's counseling is an outreach ministry for persons not members of the congregation.

One way for a pastor to develop this accountability in her parish is to ask the governing body of the church to form a small, temporary committee to assist the pastor in planning her ministry of pastoral care, particularly the ministry of pastoral counseling and referral. The initial committee might be an ad hoc rather than a standing committee so that a new pastor, when she comes to know the members of the congregation, can better change the membership of the committee in order to deal with issues that may have developed. The formation of this committee early in the pastor's ministry says that the pastor's counseling ministry is not a private practice or a secret. An important early part of the committee's initial work is, so far as possible, to advise the pastor of the "network of care" available in the community—who she should talk to about the best available help for persons in different situations.

After this initial work of establishing the counseling committee, the committee can be used to consult with and advise the pastor on a variety of situations. Should the pastor have a fund available to help people financially in certain situations? The committee can, for example, make recommendations about this and set policies so that every situation will not bring on a new decision. What kinds of situations have legal implications for pastor and congregation? The committee can support, advise, and suggest resources without in any way breaching the pastor's confidential relationship with persons. Perhaps most important, the committee provides the pastor with a sense that he or she is not working alone and that pastoral counseling is an important part of the church's ministry of pastoral care.

A Ministry of Availability

In addition to being understood as part of the congregation's ministry of pastoral care and thus accountable to the faith community, pastoral counseling can be further characterized as a ministry of availability and introduction. Although pastoral availability does not mean that pastors should have no boundaries or limits in their availability to those who ask for their help, it is of great importance to persons needing care to know that the pastor and what he represents to them is indeed available. The pastors who have trouble allowing themselves to be too available to people are those most likely to have unrealistic demands for attention placed on them.

An important and practical part of the pastor's availability is expressed through what is often called structuring. Structuring, as the term suggests, emphasizes the structure or context of the pastoral counseling. Seward Hiltner, in his book on pastoral counseling used the term "precounseling" for what is referred to here as "structuring" and in many mental health settings is called the "intake" process.[1] Whatever the terminology, it is one of the most important and most frequently neglected elements in counseling by pastors. Emphasis in a great deal of counseling training on what is and is not a good verbal response to what the counselee has said may have contributed to the neglect of training in pre-counseling or structuring.

The structuring and evaluation that should take place early in the counseling process is intended to help determine whether the counselee's concern is one that can best be addressed with the pastor or with another helping person. In this process the pastor is also assisting persons to recognize their need for help and to affirm their strength and humanness in asking for it. This recognition helps shift the focus of the counseling from being solely on the person's problem to a beginning awareness of the value of a helping relationship.

Another important part of the structuring or precounseling that should take place at the beginning of a counseling relationship is determining the most appropriate "unit of care." Can the concern that the counselee brings be dealt with most effectively individually, with both husband and wife present, or with all those who live in the household present? Having the appropriate persons involved in the counseling process is often more important than what is said in the interview. The pastor is generally better equipped to determine this than the person asking for help. Clinical training and supervision can also assist the pastor in taking responsibility for this dimension of structuring.

When the unit of care has been determined and the interview begun, one of the most useful structuring tools for the pastor is what has been called the "magic questions."[2] These questions, used in some form by virtually all the mental health disciplines, are: "What are you looking for?" "Why now?" and "Why with me?" The pastor needs to give the parishioner or counselee an opportunity to ventilate his or her concerns and thereby reduce the anxiety associated with them, but in order to understand how those concerns might be dealt with, the "magic questions" are important to order the data in an understandable way.

The first question—"What are you looking for?" or "What is painful in your life now?"—allows both parties in the relationship to focus on a particular concern. Contrary to what the pastor may feel, he or she has not been asked to deal with everything in this person's life, and the first question is a reminder of this. The second question—"Why now?"—can enable the counselee to focus the concern further. The problem probably did not always exist but began at some time and, therefore, can end or be changed or improved. The third question, "Why with me?" or "How did you decide that I was the one you wanted to talk with?" emphasizes the importance of the relationships in the process of getting help and quite naturally allows for a discussion of any previous helping relationships. Specifically identifying the pastor as the person chosen for help gives the pastor the freedom to be himself or herself and not try to imitate another type of professional helper. Recognizing from whom the parishioner has asked for help is a limiting factor on unrealistic expectations of the counseling.

Another important part of the minister's availability through structuring is some form of pastoral evaluation or diagnosis. Such an evaluation means not losing touch with the larger issues in the lives of persons in the process of attending to their specific concerns or problems. At the least this involves maintaining awareness of the kind of picture that a person paints of himself or herself and finding appropriate ways to share that in the counseling process. The pastor has a special interest in and commitment to religious concerns, but his or her ongoing diagnostic concern is in formulating ways to allow persons to see the larger picture of themselves in relation to religious and other issues. Pastoral diagnosis is not in classifying persons in a particular way, but learning to talk with them about their life story—who they have been and what they are trying to become.

Some kind of diagnosis or definition of the situation will optimally be taking place in any first interview. The concern here is that this be as usable as possible to the pastor. Even though listening is the most important skill that the pastor employs, just listening to the problem is not an adequate response for the pastoral counselor. Listening proceeds more satisfactorily if a context for listening is developed as a part of the listening. This means that the pastor should develop an active, even assertive, listening—one that is dialogical in nature. In this listening-responding style both parties in the dialogue share in the description of the parishioner's situation. This mutual involvement in the listening process is a pastor's way of "being there." Moreover, it can help avoid the most common problem for the beginning pastoral counselor, listening rather passively while a counselee dumps a problem on the pastor and then feeling the demand to come up with an "answer" to all that has been presented.

Undoubtedly the most important skill to be developed by the pastor as counselor is the capacity to offer an honest, caring relationship. It is that relationship that provides the parishioner or other counselee a direct and personal connection to the religious community and the values it represents. The pastor may or may not know a great deal about the problem that the counselee presents. In most cases, the counselee has enough knowledge to deal with the problem. What he or she usually needs is a relationship within which the resources in himself or herself that are necessary to deal with the problem can be discovered and mobilized.

The pastor's relational skill is expressed in the counseling process through hearing and understanding the counselee's story as it is presented, and in beginning to reinterpret it in terms that present the counselee as one with significant responsibility for the events of his or her life. The hearing and understanding and the reinterpreting are equally important. What the counselee says must be understood accurately enough to affirm the value of who he or she is as a person, but that problem or story needs to be enriched through the pastor's expression of what he or she has heard in the story. The counseling process is indeed dialogical. The pastor's role and function as representative of the story of faith enables him or her to reinterpret the counselee's story in the light of the faith's understanding of who a person related to God really is. This interpretive function in pastoral counseling is clearly relational.

What has been discussed thus far is the pastor's accountability and the importance of the support of the pastor's pastoral counseling ministry by the church. What has also been emphasized is the value and importance of the pastor's availability as a helping person, and the contribution of precounseling or structuring to the counseling process. What follows is a brief example of pastoral counseling that is related to the question discussed in the previous chapter about the unit of care. Although it is important that the pastor make the effort to get more than one member of a couple or family involved in the counseling, there are many times when he or she is unable to do this. Even when it is impossible to see more than one person in counseling, the pastor's work with the person who does come is facilitated because the pastor has demonstrated his or her unwillingness to enter into alliance with one family member without careful consideration of the others.

The most important thing to remember when seeing a married counselee alone—as well as in most other situations of pastoral counseling—is to insist that the counselee talk about his or her own feelings, not what is wrong with the spouse. Obviously, it is impossible to separate these completely. The counselee cannot talk about his or her own feelings without also talking about the spouse. The pastor's concern is not to rule out all material about the husband, but to get the emphasis in the most useful place on the counselee's own concerns. The dialogue that follows is with Joyce Jones, the same person discussed in the previous chapter who could not get her husband to come with her to see the pastor.

It is also a good example of some things that may be helpful in pastoral counseling whether or not it directly concerns marriage and family.[3]

Pastor: Tell me about how you happened to come in to see me. What was going on in your life that was painful?

Parishioner: My husband is never at home. He leaves at five o'clock in the morning and rarely comes home until six or seven in the evening. On the weekend he hunts or fishes. I just don't see him anymore.

Pastor: How do you feel about this?

Parishioner: I don't feel married. He doesn't seem to care about anything except being with his hunting friends. The little time he is at home he's drinking beer in front of the television.

Pastor: I'm still not sure what you are feeling about this. You sound angry.

Parishioner: I am, but I don't know what to do. Whenever I *try* to tell him how I feel, he doesn't say anything, but just walks away. And he's not doing well in his job either.

Pastor: Try to tell me what your feelings are. I hear some of your anger. You sound like you feel powerless or something like that.

Parishioner: I can't do a thing. Of course I feel powerless. What's wrong with him? That's what I want to know.

Pastor: I thought you were asking what's wrong with you.

Parishioner: There's nothing wrong with me. Or I don't think so. I'm the one who's interested in sex, not him. He's too tired or he hurt his back. There's always something to keep him away from me.

Pastor: Jerry's been successful at staying away from both of us. I don't think even my guesses about him will be very accurate unless I can get to know you better. Try to tell me how what Jerry does affects you—what kind of feelings it stirs up in you.

Parishioner: *(Long pause)* I think I feel ashamed.

The primary concern of the pastor in this interview is in getting at Joyce's pain—her feelings about her life situation. She insistently talks about what is wrong with her husband, Jerry. The pastor ignores most of this, neither asking questions about it nor reflecting on the content of what she says about him. Rather, he consistently comes back to Joyce's feelings. In reading the interview, the pastor may appear naive. Some of the things he asks seem obvious. If he is as sensitive and understanding as he is expected to be, it appears that he should know how the counselee feels. And yet if he knows or assumes he knows, Joyce will never have the opportunity to tell him who she is by saying what she feels. Everything will be a description of the "bad" husband. She and the pastor will shake their heads sadly about how bad the husband is and nothing will be done to change things.

If, however, Joyce can learn to talk about herself, to experience her own feelings, and not attribute everything important she feels to her husband, she may then begin to feel power and choice about her life. This sounds like a long process, but in just one or two encounters where her feelings rather than her husband's behavior are emphasized, she can begin to discover that there is more than one way to experience and understand her life. For the pastor this involves a rather assertive and intervening approach.

The second thing that the pastor should try to accomplish is focusing on what the counselee has done about his or her painful life situation. Feelings, awareness, and expression of what one feels lead to some differentiation from the circumstances of life and often to a sense of some power to change them. When the pastor focuses on what has been done or what the parishioner is planning to do, it furthers that process and nourishes any sense of freedom and power that may emerge. When the counselee complains about the situation or about the spouse, the pastor responds with interest in his or her action or intended action. If progress in moving from complaint to feeling has been made during the interview, the pastor can begin to respond in terms of action rather than focusing on feeling.[4] For example:

Parishioner: He was gone all weekend, and he left me a note this morning saying he wouldn't be home tonight.

Pastor: And what have you planned to do about this?

Parishioner: I don't know. I just feel so helpless.

Pastor: I think I understand something of how you feel, but I don't know yet what you are doing about those feelings.

Parishioner: Nothing, I guess. I don't know what to do.

Pastor: Well, you seem a bit clearer about how you feel about all this. That's a first step. Does he know that you've come here to get some help for yourself?

Parishioner: I don't know. I think I told him it had to do with the marriage.

Pastor: I really don't know how to be very useful to the marriage without his being here with you, so I've been assuming that what you were about was changing something about yourself. It's possible that he might be willing to come in to help you with that.

Parishioner: I'll try and tell him.

Pastor: I feel pretty sure that you can get the message across if you really want to. You've managed to share your hurt and some of your need to change with me. If you can do it here, you can eventually do it at home too.

Parishioner: How do I do it?

Pastor: I have been able to understand you when you talked about yourself and not him. I suspect that he and I are more alike than you think.

This part of the interview focuses on action—that something is being done and can be done. The counselee is offered support, but without any implicit pity, "You poor thing." The support is in the form of a reminder of what already has been done and the suggestion through implication that she can do what she needs to do. If this message comes only in words of reassurance, it will probably be rejected because it is too far removed from the counselee's way of looking at things. If, on the other hand, it is simply assumed as the way things are, the counselee may have to surrender her passivity and aggressively contradict the counselor's assumption about her competence to do what needs to be done. In either case, she has given up her stance of relating through helplessness and given the pastor new opportunity to focus on her responsibility and ability to choose.

In summary, in counseling with a married person who has been unable to get his or her spouse to participate, the pastor focuses first on the feelings of the person who is present. The strategy is valuable in almost all individual counseling. The pastor is assertive in structuring the interview so that the counselee expresses himself or herself instead of talking about the spouse or other family members who are not present. It is not possible to avoid talking about others, but the pastor can be insistent that the focus is on the person present. That focus is first on feelings and then on action, to the end that the counselee will begin to experience himself or herself as having important feelings and also the capacity for action. The pastor in this kind of counseling situation is particularly concerned to strengthen the counselee's capacities to deal with the situation in his or her life outside the counseling hour.

A Ministry of Introduction

Another important feature of the pastor's counseling ministry is assisting persons through introducing them to helping persons other than the pastor. A pastor introduces parishioners or counselee's to other professional persons because of (1) lack of time; (2) training which is insufficient or inappropriate for the situation at hand; and (3) too much involvement with the counselee or the counselee's family to allow the pastor to function professionally as well as personally.[5] Wayne Oates once described the pastor as a "minister of introduction." As such he or she introduces people to God, but "as the Christian pastor becomes durably related to persons" she "introduces them to each other and to persons who can enable them to help themselves by providing them with the rich resources that friendship, professional skills, and clinical experience can afford them."[6] The ministry of introduction, Oates says, "takes the unsightly, seemingly valueless, and even detrimental stuff of human suffering and turns it into a whole new world of significant and committed persons for the one who is in distress." Oates was concerned, as should we be, about irresponsible referrals that sometimes appear to be getting rid of someone the pastor does not know what to do with and who makes the pastor feel inadequate. It is important, therefore, to reinterpret referral in a way that reveals it as a positive ministry—a ministry of introduction.

One of the first pastoral responsibilities of a minister moving into a new community is learning the person-helping resources of that community. The community agency directory, if there is one, may be a place to start, but the pastor needs to know much more than names and phone numbers. He or she needs to know persons in those agencies so that referral may be an introduction to a person. Usually more valuable than a directory is the network of knowledge of helping persons known to the congregation and the congregation's own concern that the pastor not have to work alone.

A good referral is a ministry of introducing persons to others who can help. Only secondarily is it making them aware of agencies. In order to introduce or refer effectively, the pastor needs to know the person to whom he or she is sending a counselee. If the person to whom the counselee is referred works in an agency, the pastor needs to know something about it and its policies and advise the counselee—if this is the case—that the person to whom he or she is being referred may not be able to be his or her primary counselor. What is important, however, is that the pastor know that the professional person to whom he or she is referring a parishioner or counselee will see the person initially and be able to interpret what is to be done to respond to the counselee's need. A ministry of introduction is always person-to-person, and if the pastor finds that for some reason or another that has not been the case, he or she can take steps to see that the impersonality that the counselee has had to deal with will not happen again.

As a minister of availability as well as introduction, the pastor has time to see everyone once. Availability, however, does not mean that the pastor is obligated to continue with a counseling relationship at the cost of neglecting other significant ministerial and personal responsibilities. A pastor who has an advisory committee to consult with about his or her counseling can use that committee to consult with him or her on policies of time allotment. Certainly, the counselee should know before the session begins, or at least early in the session, that the pastor may not be with him or her personally beyond the first session and may introduce him or her to another helping person.

Good pastoral care requires that referrals be handled well. Oates has commented that when "a pastor says: 'There is nothing I can do to help you,' he has literally pronounced doom on the person, for he represents God to the person."[7] It is quite possible that the person seeking help sees the pastor as his or her last hope, not the first stop along the way to what he or she needs. The pastor who says or somehow conveys the message, "There is nothing I can do" is conveying doom, even though it is merely the pastor's own self-esteem that is requiring him or her to imply to the counselee that he or she is competent to handle most everything, but this situation is even too tough for him or her. One of the more important things a pastor can learn to do is to acknowledge limitations in a matter-of-fact rather than an emergency way. As a minister of availability, he or she is open to seeing and hearing almost anything, but he or she is not obligated by call or covenant to know how to deal with everything. Again, it is important to remember that the pastor's task is to care, not cure. If sometimes healing comes from a pastoral relationship, it is a gift of grace, not something to be demanded by either party in the relationship.

The issue of too much involvement with the counselee on an extended basis usually works out quite naturally. The pastor and the counselee are most often aware that they or their family members are related in a number of ways other than through the counseling. The pastor, therefore, can easily point out that another person would have more objectivity in looking at the situation with the counselee. Probably both the pastor and counselee feel that because of the other ways that they are related, knowing all of the details of the counselee's problem might make their relationships outside of counseling more difficult. Usually, however, that does not even need to be said in interpreting the need for introducing counselees to another helping person.

Summary and Reflection

In summary, pastoral counseling is a part of the pastoral care ministry of the church, not the private practice of the pastor. Its strength lies in the church and the pastor's availability to persons and in his or her awareness of other resources of help beyond those of the church. Pastoral counseling involves all of the wisdom that the pastor has developed in pastoral care plus the ability to structure the counseling situation through the use of questions that focus the parishioner's concerns on what he or she wants to achieve.

A Final Reflection

This book has discussed the essentials of pastoral care beginning with the theological conviction that our care of each other is based in God's care for us. The ministry of pastoral care grows out of the Christian affirmation that God created humankind for relationship with God and with God's other creatures. God continues in relationship with us by hearing and remembering us. We care for others because God cares for us. Pastoral care is not simply the act of one individual on behalf of another. It is the action of a community of faith that celebrates God's care by hearing and remembering those who are in some way cut off from the faith community.

What is essential for implementing this action is a practical, pastoral wisdom that includes what we know, what we are, and what we do. The Wisdom literature of the Bible offers insight for this because it deals more with practical human concerns than with speaking of God. Unlike other parts of ministry that involve teaching and preaching about God and religion, what is essential for pastoral care is familiarity and comfort with ordinary language about everyday life. More often than not pastoral care involves dealing with people who talk of practical, everyday problems more than they talk of God. Wisdom in pastoral care involves recognizing the deeper, theological dimension of ordinary talk whether or not God is explicitly mentioned.

The words "pastor" and "pastoral" are associated with the image and function of the shepherd and with representing the shepherd Lord described in the Twenty-third Psalm. The focus of the psalm is on the presence and guidance of the Lord in restoring the soul of those "in the darkest valley." "He restores my soul." "He leads me in right paths." "I fear no evil" because the shepherd is with me. The essential ministry of those who follow the Lord is to offer presence and guidance toward the restoring of soul.

Restoring soul to those who are in some way lost or separated from the community of faith is far more than a role to play or a function to perform. Theologically, a pastoral carer, whether laity or clergy, is not called to care for persons by solving their problems. He or she is called to recognize and communicate, even in the most difficult circumstances, that a person is more than the problem he or she presents. The patient or parishioner is not just a medical or psychological diagnosis, a couple struggling to stay in a painful marriage, a lonely or demoralized person.

Those for whom the pastor cares are persons created for relationship with God and God's creation. The pastor may contribute to the solution of the person's problem, but the pastoral care offered is not the guidance given but the relationship provided and the restoring of soul that can result from that. Rediscovering one's self and one's power to live and to change in the context of relationship is what pastoral care is all about. Care is pastoral when it looks deeper than the immediate circumstances of a person's life and reminds that person that he or she is a child of God created in and for relationship.

Notes

1. Pastoral Wisdom

1. Carol A. Newsom, "Wisdom Tradition, Biblical," in *Dictionary of Pastoral Care and Counseling*, ed. Rodney J. Hunter (Nashville: Abingdon Press, 1990), p. 1326.

2. This interpretation of Kierkegaard's concept of repetition may be found in John D. Caputo's *Radical Hermeneutics* (Bloomington: Indiana University Press, 1987) and in Romney C. Moseley's *Becoming a Self Before God* (Nashville: Abingdon Press, 1991), pp. 62-63.

3. John Macmurray, *The Self as Agent* (New York: Harper and Brothers, 1957), p. 38.

4. John Macmurray, *Persons in Relation* (New York: Harper and Brothers, 1961), p. 17.

5. Ibid., pp. 157-58.

6. Paul W. Pruyser, "A Transformational Understanding of Humanity," *Changing Views of the Human Condition*, ed. Paul W. Pruyser (Macon, Ga.: Mercer University Press, 1987), pp. 4-8.

2. Pastoral Presence

1. David Duncombe, "Christian Life," in *Dictionary of Pastoral Care and Counseling*, ed. Rodney J. Hunter (Nashville: Abingdon Press, 1990), pp. 148-49.

2. Walter Brueggemann, *Theology of the Old Testament* (Minneapolis: Fortress Press, 1997), pp. 317-403.

3. Pastoral Guidance

1. Seward Hiltner, *Preface to Pastoral Theology* (Nashville: Abingdon Press, 1958), pp. 145-74.
2. Reinhold Niebuhr, *Leaves from the Notebook of a Tamed Cynic* (New York: Meridian Books, 1957), p. 21.
3. Eugene Gendlin, "Client-Centered Therapy: A Current View," in David A. Wexler and Laura North Rice, *Innovations in Client-Centered Therapy* (New York: John Wiley & Sons, 1974), p. 217.

4. Limit, Loss, and Grief

1. Judith Viorst, *Necessary Losses* (New York: Simon and Schuster, 1986).
2. Karl Barth, *Church Dogmatics,* vol. III, part 2 (Edinburgh: T. & T. Clark, 1960), pp. 514-73.
3. Ibid.
4. Sigmund Freud, "Mourning and Melancholia," in *Collected Papers,* vol. IV (London: The Hogarth Press, 1956), pp. 152-70.
5. Robert J. Lifton, preface to *The Inability to Mourn,* by Arthur Mitscherlich and M. Mitscherlich (New York: Grove Press, 1975), p. vii.
6. Granger Westberg, *Good Grief* (Philadelphia: Fortress Press, 1971).
7. Elisabeth Kübler-Ross, *On Death and Dying* (New York: Macmillan, 1969).
8. Larry R. Churchill, "The Human Experience of Dying: The Moral Primacy of Stories Over Stages," *Soundings* 62 (Spring 1979): 35-36.
9. Vanderlyn R. Pine, ed., *Unrecognized and Unsanctioned Grief* (Springfield, Ill.: Charles C. Thomas, 1990) and Kenneth J. Doka, ed., *Disenfranchised Grief: Recognizing Hidden Sorrow* (Lexington, Mass.: Lexington Books, 1989).
10. Thomas Attig, *How We Grieve: Relearning the World* (New York: Oxford University Press, 1996).
11. Ibid., p. 7.
12. Ibid., p. 46.
13. Ibid., p. 56.
14. Ibid., p. 107.
15. Ibid., pp. 170-91.
16. C. S. Lewis, *A Grief Observed* (San Francisco: Harper & Row, 1989), p. 63.
17. John Patton, "Your 'Present and Silence,' " editorial in *The Journal of Pastoral Care* 26, no. 2 (June 1972): 73. Used by permission.

18. Kathleen O'Connor, *Lamentations and the Tears of the World* (Marynoll, N.Y.: Orbis Books, 2003), p. 9.

19. Ibid., p. 94.

20. Daniel L. Migliore, "Death, Meaning of (Christian)," in *Dictionary of Pastoral Care and Counseling,* ed. Rodney J. Hunter (Nashville: Abingdon Press, 1990), pp. 261-62.

21. Jürgen Moltmann, "Eschatology and Pastoral Care," in *Dictionary of Pastoral Care and Counseling* (Nashville: Abingdon Press, 1990), pp. 361-62.

22. Jerome D. Frank and Julia B. Frank, *Persuasion and Healing,* 3rd ed. (Baltimore: Johns Hopkins University Press, 1993), pp. 34-39.

5. Care for the Sick

1. Eric Partridge, *Origins: A Short Etymological Dictionary of Modern English* (New York: Macmillan, 1966), p. 475.

2. Susan Sontag, *Illness as Metaphor* and *AIDS and Its Metaphors* (New York: Anchor, 1990), p. 3.

3. Liston O. Mills, "Hospitalization, Experience Of," in *Dictionary of Pastoral Care and Counseling,* ed. Rodney J. Hunter (Nashville: Abingdon Press, 1990), p. 538.

4. John Patton, "Hospital Visitation," in *Dictionary of Pastoral Care and Counseling,* pp. 537-38.

5. Elaine Scarry, *The Body in Pain* (New York: Oxford University Press, 1985), p. 4.

6. Arthur Kleinman, *The Illness Narratives* (New York: Basic Books, 1988), p. 26.

7. E. Cassell, "Life as a Work of Art," *The Hastings Center Report* 14, no. 5 (1984): 35-37.

8. Arthur Frank, *At the Will of the Body: Reflections on Illness* (Boston: Houghton Mifflin Co., 1991), pp. 40-41.

9. Ibid., p. 128.

10. Warren Thomas Reich, "Speaking of Suffering: A Moral Account of Compassion," *Soundings* 72, no. 1 (Spring 1989): 89.

11. Ibid., pp. 88-90.

6. Abuse of Self and Others

1. James B. Nelson, *Thirst: God and the Alcoholic Experience* (Louisville: Westminster John Knox Press, 2004), pp. 41-42.

2. Roland C. Summit, "The Child Sexual Abuse Accommodation Syndrome," *Child Abuse and Neglect*, vol. 7: 177-93.

3. See Marie Fortune's early work on sexual abuse, *Sexual Violence* (New York: Pilgrim Press, 1983). More recent information may be obtained from The Center for the Prevention of Sexual and Domestic Violence in Seattle, Washington, now known as the FaithTrust Institute.

4. James Newton Poling, *The Abuse of Power: A Theological Problem* (Nashville: Abingdon Press, 1991), p. 69.

5. Merle A. Fossum and Marilyn J. Mason, *Facing Shame: Families in Recovery* (New York: W. W. Norton & Company, 1986), p. 79.

6. On the issue of confidentiality see Sissela Bok, "The Limits of Confidentiality," *A Hastings Center Report* (February 1983): 24-25.

7. Mary D. Pellauer, Barbara Chester, and Jane A. Boyajian, *Sexual Assault and Abuse* (San Francisco: Harper & Row, 1987), p. xi.

8. See Karen Lebacqz, *Professional Ethics: Power and Paradox* (Nashville: Abingdon Press, 1985) and Karen Lebacqz and Ronald G. Barton, *Sex in the Parish* (Louisville: Westminster/John Knox, 1991).

7. Care of Marriage and Family

1. Lyman Wynne and Adele Wynne, "The Quest for Intimacy," *Journal of Marital and Family Therapy* 12, no. 4 (1986): 383-94.

2. Peter Berger, *Facing Up to Modernity: Excursions in Society, Politics, and Religion* (New York: Basic Books, 1977), pp. 7-10.

3. Thomas Patrick Malone and Patrick Thomas Malone, *The Art of Intimacy* (New York: Prentice Hall Press, 1987), pp. 25-29.

8. Pastoral Counseling

1. Seward Hiltner, *Pastoral Counseling* (New York: Abingdon Press, 1949), pp. 125-48.

2. John Patton, *Pastoral Counseling: A Ministry of the Church* (Nashville: Abingdon Press, 1983), pp. 83-93.

3. Ibid., pp. 100-101.

4. Ibid., pp. 102-3.

5. Ibid., pp. 164-66.

6. Wayne Edward Oates, *The Christian Pastor*, 3rd ed. (Philadelphia: Westminster Press, 1982), p. 262.

7. Ibid., p. 278.